On The Trail
Of Liberation

A RECOUNTING OF
PRECIOUS MOMENTS WITH AMMA

Edited by Br. Madhavamrita Chaitanya

ON THE TRAIL OF LIBERATION
A RECOUNTING OF PRECIOUS MOMENTS WITH AMMA

Edited by Br. Madhavamrita Chaitanya

Published by:
Mata Amritanandamayi Center
P.O. Box 613
San Ramon, CA 94583-0613, USA
Website: www.amma.org

In India:
www.amritapuri.org
inform@amritapuri.org

In Europe:
www.amma-europe.org

In US:
www.amma.org

CONTENTS

FOREWORD

For the disciples of a unique and genuine spiritual master—someone established in *sahaja-samadhi* (constant abidance in highest state of awareness)—illustrating their first-hand experiences with the guru is an attempt to express the inexpressible. Yet, this is exactly what has been going on in Amritapuri—the abode of Amma, Sri Mata Amritanandamayi Devi—for the last year and a half, during the corona-pandemic lockdown.

The fundamental principle of Sanatana Dharma, the Hindu faith, is all-inclusiveness. It advocates many paths and forms to ensure none are excluded and to provide a full palette of choices for its seekers and followers. As Amma says, "One path will not suit everyone, as the nature of people's minds and their inherent tendencies are different. Insisting on one path is like promoting only one size and model of shoes." So, in fact, Hinduism is monotheistic. It believes in a single, undivided, supreme reality—Brahman—the one and only truth, the very substratum of this manifested world of name and form.

Amma follows this ancient lineage of the *rishis*. She accepts everyone and all paths—*karma*, *bhakti* and *jnana*—and discards nothing. Therefore, in this compilation of talks, you will see a beautiful blend of devotion, selfless action and Vedantic knowledge.

These talks and their wide-ranging insights and experiences provide much to reflect upon. They present us with an opportunity to better understand and internalize the mystery that is Amma, as well as a gateway to access wisdom rooted in the personal, internal growth that accompanies spirituality and a close relationship with a living guru. As the stories unfold, an unambiguous path unlocking the doors of your heart is revealed through an incessant flow of divine experiences, thought-provoking lessons and meditative moments.

The key is love—the unbroken stream of pure unconditional love that flows from Amma to one and all. Amma's love manifests as a full circle, embracing everyone and continuously circling back—"a real meeting of hearts," as Amma puts it. The 'negative' experience of the coronavirus lockdown has spawned a transformation at Amritapuri—a 'celebration,' if you will, the divine and blissful experience of everyone's stories being shared. Through this, everyone has developed a deeper understanding of the depth of Amma's knowledge and its impact on the world.

It would not be an exaggeration in any way if I were to say that this compilation is a treasure—a priceless gift from Amma to her children all over the world. It is not a mere collection of experiences, but an excellent reference book providing a glimpse of true spirituality. It presents the vast expressions of the genuine guru-disciple relationship as envisaged and maintained by the ancient sages of India. It is a guide for spiritual seekers, an elixir to instill self-confidence, determination and detachment as the seeker faces internal and external challenges, and almost an encyclopedia of ways in which seekers have used Amma's teachings to overcome the constant confusion created by the mind.

Each talk has references and stories from the Vedas, Upanishads, *Bhagavad Gita, Brahma Sutras*, Puranas and Itihasas, etc. Besides the sannyasis, brahmacharis and brahmacharinis, other ashram residents—including householder devotees and professors and researchers serving in the various schools of

Amrita University—have participated. Hence, some of the talks are elucidated with scientific and logical references to clarify the perspective of the speaker.

For one and a half years now—since the commencement of the pandemic—the live international webcasts from Amritapuri have been the only solace and refuge for Amma's children all over the world. Complete with Amma's meditation, bhajans, talks by the ashram residents seated beside Amma, and Amma's own messages and question-and-answer sessions, these daily webcasts have been tremendously enriching, instilling devotees with the self-confidence, faith and courage required to cope in these trying times. Through these programs, the physical gap between the devotees and Amma has been as if removed. The devotees are able to experience Amma's presence and protection. Every day they have something to inspire them to remain patient, fearless and peaceful.

In the Amritapuri Ashram, these pandemic days have been filled with ongoing Sanskrit and scriptural classes, discussions based on those classes, meditation, 'Ma-Om Meditation' and 'White Flower Meditation,' followed by bhajans, question-and-answer sessions with Amma and much more. The Amritapuri Ashram is a huge community—a conglomeration of people from around the world, including sannyasis, brahmacharis, brahmacharinis and families. Every single person, from little children to adults, is being provided the opportunity to talk and discuss. Usually, Amma gives them a topic, with Amma Herself elaborating at the end in her own simple, descriptive manner. As a whole, it is an inspiring spiritual feast.

The talks included in this book are not merely beneficial for spiritual seekers. They can shed light on all spheres of life, regardless of one's profession, nationality, language or religious faith. As the residents open their heart, the readers will also feel their heart opening. It is like beholding the enthralling beauty of a bud blossoming into a flower. Each of these speeches has a personal aspect because the speakers share some of their personal struggles, family situations, inner conflicts, the way they lived life before meeting Amma, and how a change in perspective occurred due to Amma's influence. The talks will also help you learn how to overcome some of your own weaknesses — things you consider as stumbling blocks on your path. If your heart is open enough, you can gain insight into how to change things you have always believed to be 'impossible to change.' Don't be surprised if you see yourself in some of the speakers.

During this period of introspection, more and more of the ashram residents are realizing the value of breaking the shackles of the limited 'I' — the false notion that "I am this finite body, mind and ego." Once that bond snaps, the all-pervading 'I-ness' — the oneness, the essence of your true being — shines forth. In that absolute state of existence, nothing is separate from you. You are in everything, and everything is in you. There is a beautiful bhajan written and composed by Amma, in which she reveals this highest realization in simple words: *"annutott-anyamayi kanan kazhiññilla ellam-entatmavennorttu"* — "From that moment onwards, I couldn't see anything as separate from me. I remembered everything as my own Self."

As Uddalaka says to his son, Shvetaketu, in Chandogya Upanishad, 6.1.3: *"yenashrutam shrutam bhavatyamatam matam-avijñatam vijñatam-iti katham nu bhagavah sa adesho bhavatiti"* — "That teaching by which what is never heard becomes heard, what is never thought of becomes thought of, what is never known becomes known." This indeed is the knowledge in which Amma eternally abides: "That by knowing which everything is known."

This 'knowing' explains the attraction and inexplicable bond that all of us have with Amma. One of the most uplifting, heart-warming and fulfilling experiences is watching the way Amma is grooming the little children in the ashram. Amma's understanding of the world, people and other living beings is incomparable. Needless to say, Amma understands children better than anyone else. The way these children respond to Amma's questions — their devotion and loving connection with Amma and their eagerness to learn the scriptures — cannot be put into words. As is said, "You have to see it to believe it."

Allow me to recall Amma's words, "The Sanskrit word, *'samskara'* (deep-seated impressions carried from previous lives), is usually translated as 'culture.' However, the word 'culture' also refers to 'culturing' a small sample of our blood or sputum in a lab, where an optimal environment is created for the bacteria in the sample to grow. It is the same with 'culture,' when it refers to inner growth. In order for our children to thrive, we first need to create a conducive atmosphere at home and then later at school." Amma not only teaches; she translates every single word she utters into action. So, it goes without saying that every moment Amma creates an atmosphere for her children to remember and contemplate on the sphere of the *atma* — the 'atma-sphere.' In that most conducive atmosphere, spiritual blossoming simply takes place.

I sincerely hope that these personal experiences told by people who journeyed through the inner and outer worlds — the subjective and objective realms, the spiritual and emotional planes — kindle at least a small flame in your heart, shedding light on the path of your quest to reality.

Swami Amritaswarupananda
Amritapuri Ashram, May 1, 2021

PREFACE

Om amriteshwaryai namah. When the lockdown was imposed in March 2020 in response to the COVID-19 pandemic, Amma asked ashram residents to prepare *satsangs* (spiritual discourses). She said that doing so would help them take stock of their ashram life and reflect on spiritual matters. This led to the launch of a series of talks held almost every evening in Amritapuri. The talks were a generous sharing of the speakers' experiences with Amma. Thus, the satsangs lived up to the meaning of the word: *sat-sangha*, or companionship with truth.

The speakers, initially the ashram's monastics, were asked to speak on scriptural topics assigned to them. Most of the topics were celebrated verses from the scriptures, particularly the *Bhagavad Gita*. One would have imagined then that the talks would be scholarly, with speakers sharing their insights into the scriptures. They were not, for the swamis and swaminis, brahmacharis and brahmacharinis spoke not as pundits but as Amma's children. As far as they were concerned, what they had experienced with and learnt from her were primary; the scriptures merely affirmed those learnings.

One speaker illustrated it humorously with an anecdote. A student preparing for an examination studied cows thoroughly. But the exam question turned out to be about coconut trees. The candidate who knew nothing about them wrote reams about cows, and ended by noting that they were tied to coconut trees. In the same way, no matter what Amma's children are asked to speak about, they inevitably end up talking about her.

This does not negate the scriptures. On the contrary, when the scriptural texts are refracted through the prism of personal experience, they become more meaningful and relevant. In this way, Amma ensures that scriptures are not perceived as abstractions but seen for what they really are: the bedrock truths of life.

As a Guru, her primary tool of teaching is not the classroom but the crucible of circumstance, custom-made for each disciple. Hence, it should come as no surprise when a brahmacharini or swamini serving as a principal in one of the ashram's schools waxes lyrical about how Amma's unseen guidance taught her to work as an instrument in the hands of the Guru; when a brahmachari supervising kitchen operations marvels at Amma's culinary expertise and management skills; or when yet another monastic's reminiscence of how Amma freed him from the clutches of addiction and terminal disease is tinged with wonder and reverence.

In other words, the work that Amma assigned them became their primer on *sadhana* (spiritual practice), *sharanagati* (self-surrender), *shraddha* (attentiveness and faith) and the Guru's *sarvajnatva* (omniscience), among other spiritual principles. In this way, she helped them see age-old scriptural doctrines in a new light.

Soon after the talks began, many ashram residents, both monastics and householders, repeatedly asked how they could avail themselves of these talks, which they found so inspiring, relevant and beneficial to their own spiritual lives, and which they felt would constitute an archive of ashram life. This is how the idea of compiling the satsangs was born.

For the speakers, preparing these talks was a meditation on Amma. Giving them while seated next to her was yet another unforgettable experience. And listening to her children was joyful for Amma. We hope that this first volume of talks will also delight you, dear reader, and deepen your devotion and dedication to Amma.

Br. Madhavamrita Chaitanya

1

In Her Shelter
Swami Akshayamritananda Puri

The whole world has been affected by the coronavirus pandemic. Residents of the Amritapuri Ashram are fortunate to be able to live in close proximity to Amma without having to face the problems that people outside encounter. When devotees call and tell me about the problems they are facing, I am reminded of how safe we are. Amma is taking such good care of each one of us.

She has created congenial circumstances for us to make the most of the lockdown period to uplift ourselves spiritually. One of the new features of this period has been *satsangs* (spiritual talks) in Amritapuri. Preparing for them makes us reflect on the spiritual lessons we have learned. Listening to them makes us think constantly about Amma and the relevance of scriptural teachings in our lives.

Before a rocket is launched, a booster rocket is attached to it. Without this booster, the spacecraft cannot break free from earth's orbit and enter space. This satsang series is one of many such booster rockets that Amma has put in place to help us in our journey of life.

From the day we receive the satsang topic, the thought about speaking in Amma's presence leads us to a state of meditation even without our knowing about it.

Before joining the ashram, I used to take part in the activities of the Kozhikode Ashram for many years. I was in charge of AYUDH, Amma's youth wing, for six years. When I was going to join the ashram, Amma's children in Kozhikode threw a big farewell party for me. After the party, they sent me off at the railway station. They said, "Giri, we've come to send you off to remind you about something important: you are going to Amma. You should not come back for any reason. You should become the pride of Kozhikode!"

I replied, "I'm prepared to do whatever I'm asked to do in the ashram... anything except give satsangs! I hope I'll be allowed to skip that!"

Two months after joining the ashram, Amma asked everyone to give satsangs. As soon as I heard this, I started hiding from Amritageetananda Swami, who assigned satsang topics. One day, when I was standing near the toilet, I saw Swami coming there. I immediately went into the toilet and locked myself inside. I remained there for about an hour just to escape from him! But eventually, he caught me. He handed me a piece of paper with my satsang topic. I panicked! But when I recalled the faces of the Kozhikode devotees who had come to send me off, I felt that I could not leave the ashram; I did not want to leave either.

I began to think about the topic. I thought about it all the time, even while in the toilet. Slowly, some ideas began to crop up in my mind. Eventually, I gave my first ever satsang in front of Amma. After that, when I went to see Amma, she told me that she liked my satsang. That word of praise from Amma remains my inspiration to give satsangs even today.

Amma is a living Upanishad. Her life and actions show us what *sadhana* (spiritual practice) is and how to do it. Her every word and deed are spiritual teachings. Through our different experiences in life, Amma imparts scriptural knowledge.

I was born and raised in a famous place in Kerala. No, it is not Guruvayoor or Chottanikkara, but Kuthiravattam in Kozhikode. The house I lived in is just 200 meters from the Kuthiravattam Mental Hospital!

Many notable literary and artistic figures—like Kuthiravattam Pappu, Thikkodiyan, Nellikode Bhaskaran, S.K. Pottekkatt and Balan K. Nair—were born here. Kuthiravattam also houses a library that has twice won the State Award for Best Library in Kerala.

My friends were the children of some of the richest people in Kozhikode. Our motto in life was to make merry and live life to the fullest. One or two hours a week in college, five movies a week, and tours on weekends—such was our way of life. It was a time of enjoyment with no thought of the future.

During this time, a relative came to me with a problem related to his younger brother, Das. He said, "Das has fallen into a trap. He does not come home much now and does not go to work regularly. He stays somewhere in Kayamkulam during his holidays and says that he is going to see an Amma. She is just 32 years old and sings bhajans. When she sings, she sounds intoxicated, and is always surrounded by many young men. Giri, you have to save him somehow!"

I promised him that I would. The next day, I called Das and told him to come to my house. When he arrived, I observed a change in his behavior. I asked him, "How can you call someone who isn't much older than you, Amma? Why look for another mother when you have a good mother at home? Do we need more than one mother in our life?"

When I finished asking all my questions, he enthusiastically started to speak about Amma, not stopping even for a moment. I found many of the things he said hard to believe. No matter how much I tried to make Das see reason, I could not cure him of his madness for Amma. Not only that, he insisted that I visit Amma. I told him, "I have a mother of my own. I don't need any other mother!"

One day, Das called me and said, "Amma is coming to Kodungallur. You must come along with me!"

Thinking that this would be an opportunity to stop his Amma madness, I told him that I would. Thus, on April 12, 1986, we set out for Kodungallur. April 14th was *Vishu*.[1] In those days, missing Vishu festivities was unthinkable. I agreed to see Amma on the condition that we would return that very day.

Amma's program was held at the Kodungallur Sharada Bhakta Samaj. We arrived there in the evening. Several people were waiting in front of the hall to receive Amma. Suddenly, a vehicle drove up and stopped before us. Amma got out. In the rush of devotees, we could not see her properly. We went to the front of the hall. Amma arrived on the stage. I was closely observing her every move. I thought, "There's something special about the way she laughs and talks. No wonder Das spoke so highly of her!"

Amma started singing bhajans. Her melodious voice was heart-warming. The first song was *'Gajanana he gajanana'* and the next was *'Gopalakrishna radha krishna.'* From a young age, I have had a keen interest in music. My main hobby was singing old Malayalam film songs to my friends. I enjoyed Amma's bhajans immensely. Each bhajan gave me goose pimples. Though I had attended many concerts before, I had never before perceived the divinity that was palpable in Amma's voice. I forgot myself and became immersed in the entrancing power of her singing.

One bhajan that Amma sang touched me deeply: *'Bandhamilla bandhuvilla svantam allonnum...'* — 'No one is ours. There is nothing we can call our own...'

---

[1] A festival celebrated by Malayalee Hindus as the New Year.

This song unsettled me profoundly. Perhaps it might even have inspired the change in my life. I don't know how those two hours passed. For the first time in my life, I felt as if I was getting intoxicated without liquor.

Amma's bhajans were followed by darshan. When I reached Amma, she asked me, "Where are you from?"

"Kozhikode," I said.

Amma caressed my chest gently. I couldn't say anything. I even forgot to talk about Das, for I was still feeling intoxicated. I continued to remain there, watching Amma, until darshan ended and Amma left.

When we learned that she was going to visit a devotee's house, we followed her. We thoroughly enjoyed watching Amma being received by the family and seeing the way she spoke to them.

The swamis who had accompanied Amma went to a nearby temple to perform a *Harikatha*.[2] Amma went to sit on a sand dune in the courtyard of the house. All the devotees sat in front of her. Most of them were young people. Many of them asked her questions. Amma gave clear answers to all of them. I was sitting silently by her side. Amma spoke about the changes that were likely to take place in the world in 25 years. She spoke about political issues and the abuse of alcohol and drugs among young people. At that time, Amma specifically mentioned the need for young people to perform austerities. I felt as if everything Amma said was about me; all her words were meant for me alone.

After the Harikatha, the swamis returned and Amma got into a vehicle with them. Suddenly, she came back and said, "Call the children from Kozhikode." With a pounding heart, I went near Amma. She asked me where Das was. I told her that he was sleeping. Amma said that he had a bad headache and

---

[2] Literally, 'Story of Hari' (Lord Vishnu). A traditional form of discourse in which the narration is interspersed with singing.

that we should not disturb him. Das did not tell me that he had a headache. Later, when I asked him, he confirmed that he had been suffering from a headache, but that he had not told Amma about it.

Amma caressed my chest once again and asked me, "Aren't you coming to Vallikkavu?"

I nodded my head and said, "I will come, Amma." Thus, for the first time, I called her Amma. When her vehicle started moving away, I stood there watching it disappear. I felt as if my connection with Amma was age-old.

When Das woke up, I told him that Amma had asked if we were going to Vallikkavu. I said that we could always return home after going to Vallikkavu. I was no longer concerned about Vishu festivities or my friends.

Das and I went straight to Amritapuri. When we reached the ashram, I was so entranced by its charming atmosphere that I started singing, *"Svarggattekkal sundaraman i svapnam viriyum gramam, premamayiyam ente amma tamasikkum gramam"*—"This dream village—where my mother, the embodiment of love, lives—is more beautiful than heaven."

Amma walked towards us and took us to a grove of coconut trees. We sat under a coconut tree. There were only the three of us. Amma spoke to us for a long while. She then got up saying that we could leave after bhava darshan in the evening.

Amma's bhava darshan began after the evening bhajans. When the door of the *kalari* opened, we saw a different Amma. We have a famous family temple in Kozhikode, the Azhakodi Devi Temple. When I saw Amma in Devi Bhava, I felt as if the Azhakodi Devi, a form of the Goddess, was standing before me. Amma visited this temple twice later, and it was there that many of those from Kozhikode who are now ashram residents first saw Amma.

At that time, I was facing a problem at home. My brother's wife had a strange illness. The two of them had been married for only 10 months at that time. We learned about the disease only during her pregnancy. As there was no treatment available in Kozhikode, my brother and his wife had gone to Vellore. The baby was due in the first week of May. Doctors said that my sister-in-law had only a 2% chance of survival. When I told Amma about this during the Devi Bhava darshan, she listened to me, poured water into my mouth, and pressed her finger in the middle of my forehead. I felt something like an electric shock. Amma then declared, "Nothing will happen. Amma will make a firm resolve. Be strong, my son."

The next morning, we boarded the train for Kozhikode. I do not know how I reached home, for my mind was fully engrossed with thoughts of Amma. The first thing I did when I got home was to put a photo of Amma in a room and turn that room into a prayer room.

On April 20, my brother called me from Vellore to let me know that his wife had given birth without any problem. Both mother and child were fine. When they came back home and saw the photo of Amma, they told me that the person in this photo had come to the hospital that day. I was astonished! I realized that everything Das had said about Amma was true. Amma is none other than Devi herself. Today, Das is also an ashram resident, now known as Br. Nirvanamrita Chaitanya.

Despite all these experiences and despite my love for and devotion to Amma, my character did not change much. My life continued on the twin tracks of devotion to Amma on one side and friends and related activities on the other.

Shortly afterward, Amma came to Kozhikode. When I went for darshan, my mother also came with me. I knew that she wanted to tell Amma about my bad habits! So, I left her in the darshan queue and joined the queue only much later. When I reached Amma, I saw my mother sitting by her side. She must have already told Amma about me. During darshan, I told Amma that I wanted to serve her by staying with her. Amma told me to come to Vallikkavu and said that she would give me a mantra.

When I went to Vallikkavu, I experienced Amma's omniscience again. A swamini gave Amma a piece of paper on which the mantra was written. Seeing it, Amma pulled her ear and said, "This is not his mantra! Change it!" I never told Amma who my *ishta devata* (favorite deity) was, or what mantra I wanted.

Every year on the eve of Onam,[3] the club I was a member of would treat the patients of Kuthiravattam Mental Hospital to a lavish Onam feast. The function would be attended by district collectors and ministers.

After the Onam feast, my friends and I would usually go to a fancy restaurant to party. That year, we did the same. We sat outside on the lawn to enjoy our mugs of beer. But for some reason, I just could not drink it. Whenever I brought the mug to my mouth, Amma's face would appear in my mind. No matter how many times I tried, I was unable to drink. My hands started trembling. I then poured the alcohol on the ground and took a vow mentally, even as I beheld Amma's face in my mind: "I will never again touch alcohol!" After this incident, my life changed completely. When I went to see Amma on her 33rd birthday, I was a new person.

I started doing seva full time at the Kozhikode Ashram. I participated in the construction of the ashram and Brahmasthanam Temple and the local Amrita Vidyalayam school. Whenever senior disciples from the ashram came to the Malabar region, I would accompany them, play the harmonium and sing bhajans with them, and take part in AYUDH and other activities. I

---

[3] The biggest festival in Kerala, practically its national festival. It occurs in the month of Chingam (August – September).

wanted to join the Amritapuri ashram but my mother threatened to kill herself if I did so.

After the consecration of the Kozhikode Brahmasthanam Temple, Amma called all the volunteers for darshan. She asked me, "Have you decided? What did your mother say?" When I told Amma that she was against my staying in the ashram, Amma said, "Just come to the ashram. I'll take care of your mother."

A week later, when the committee members of the Kozhikode Ashram went to Amritapuri, Amma asked me, "Have you come prepared to stay here?" I had not. Amma's question upset me a lot. When I reached home, I told my mother firmly, "I'm going to join the ashram!" Contrary to my expectation, my mother did not object. Thus, I joined the ashram and became a member of Amma's ashram family.

Kuthiravattam Pappu, one of the greatest comedians in Malayalam cinema, was a close friend. Pappu was a communist and an atheist. I invited him many times to meet Amma. He not only refused but would also retort, "Don't you have anything better to do?" At that time, his star was shining brightly. Malayalees adored him and his very name used to bring a smile to their faces. All of a sudden, he contracted a deadly disease and had to be hospitalized for months. He was unable to act. In a short period of time, the life of this man took a drastic turn for the worse. From a happy and comfortable life, he slipped into a state of sheer helplessness. This change had a deep impact on me and made me reflect on the fragility of life.

After he recovered, he went to see Amma when she came to Kozhikode. Amma hugged him and asked about his health. She held him close to her. He spoke to Amma for a long time. She whispered something in his ears, and he started to laugh.

I went to see him again after the Brahmasthanam festival. I noticed a change in him. I asked him how he felt after meeting

Amma and whether his opinion had changed. His eyes welled up with tears and he could not speak for a while. He then said, "I'm the one who made Malayalees all over the world laugh. Many celebrities comforted me in person and over the phone when I fell ill. But it was Amma who made me laugh again when I was exhausted and unable to laugh anymore. There are many mothers in the movies. They all act well, but this mother is like the mother who gave birth to us. When I saw Amma, I felt happier than I had while acting in hundreds of movies. It was when I was in her lap that my 'Pappu' nature — my ability to laugh and to make others laugh — was truly restored."

He told me that he had asked Amma for two things that day: "I've not been sleeping properly for months, Amma, and I really want to sleep well. I also wish to act in at least one more movie before I die." He continued, "After that day, I started sleeping well again. Two days later, the famous movie director, I.V. Shashi, called me with an offer for a new movie. The next day, another famous director, Hariharan, called with an offer for a role in one of his films. After telling Amma that I wish to act in a movie, I got two offers within three or four days." He then told me to convey his heartfelt greetings to Amma.

A year-and-a-half after I joined the ashram, Amma sent me to Wayanad. Wayanad then was very different. Having been born and raised in the heart of Kozhikode city, it was a whole new world for me. Many people were poor, and they included the *adivasis* (aborigines), who were being exploited by anti-social elements and evangelists.

More than this, what struck me was the influence Amma had on people there. She had visited the place several times and the local ashram was thriving even without the presence of an ashram representative. Amma has even held a public program in Mananthavady (which Amma calls 'Anandavadi' or 'Garden of

Happiness') when there was no one from the ashram to coordinate programs.

In those days, the main activity of ashram representatives was making house calls. We used to visit an average of 25 – 30 houses every day. There was no one who did not know Amma, even in the most remote villages. People showed us tremendous respect when we said that we were from Amma's ashram. They also shared many experiences they had with Amma.

Hearing the experiences of hundreds of her devotees, I realized that Amma had sent me to Wayanad not to uplift the people there, but to revive and heal me. I believe that it is purely because of Amma's immense grace that I have become a tool for carrying out Amma's work among them for the last 25 years, thus helping me to smooth my rough edges. ☙

2

Cultivating Devotion
Swami Anaghamritananda Puri

Let me briefly share how I became a devotee of Amma. As she would have put it, I am one of those "who changed after meeting Amma."

In those days, I had gained a misguided understanding of spiritually inclined people from articles that levelled scurrilous allegations against them. I never bothered to check if the allegations were true or false and never associated with ashrams in general. However, I had a nodding acquaintance with the Sri Ramakrishna Seva Ashram at Kaloor, Ernakulam. I also attended talks by pundits like Vaidyalinga Sharma, Narayana Pisharody, Prema Pandurangan and Madhavji.

Despite my misgivings about 'spiritual people,' I admired three sannyasis. One was Swami Vivekananda, whom Indians love and revere. The other two were Swami Jayendra Saraswathi of the Kanchi Math and Swami Vishwesha Thirtha of the Pejawar Math. I had met them both. Their words and demeanor attracted me greatly.

I used to visit the Pavakulam Sree Mahadeva Temple. Once, when I went there, I saw a flyer featuring a photograph of a woman. I asked someone about the flyer, and he told me that the flyer belonged to Ravi-chettan,[4] and the photo was that of

---

[4] A devotee of Amma. 'Chettan' means 'older brother' in Malayalam, and is often added as a suffix when addressing older males, as a mark of respect.

Amma. In the photo, Amma is in the *kalari*, and both her hands are on her chest. I found this picture captivating.

Two days later, I met Ravi-chettan and asked him who Amma was. To my shock, he began to cry profusely. He then started speaking at length about Amma, all the while trying to suppress his sobs. He said that Amma was Parashakti, the Almighty, and that she has performed miracles. If she has met someone once, she will remember that person thereafter. I did not think there was anything special about that. The defamatory articles I had read earlier were still on my mind. However, the next few sentences Ravi-chettan spoke inspired me to meet Amma. He said, "Everyone is equal to Amma. She does not discriminate against anyone. She loves everyone equally."

Those words sank deep into my mind, where they continued to resound over and over again. I felt that loving everyone equally was impossible for human beings. If Amma could do so, there must be something special about her and I wanted to meet her.

Even without my asking, Ravi-chettan volunteered to take me to Amma. But he went to Amritapuri several times afterwards without taking me. When I asked him why, he explained that the thought of visiting Amma would occur to him suddenly, whereupon he would act on that whim at once, and would have no time to inform me or anyone else. I did not believe him then, but later, I realized it was true when I started acting in the same way also.

One day, Ravi-chettan told me, "You needn't go to Amritapuri. Amma's coming here!"

The Pavakulam temple committee had formally invited her. So, one day in 1986, Amma was accorded a welcome at the temple. When Amma's bhajans began, her sweet and soulful voice evoked deep devotion in me. After bhajans, I returned home, as I did not like crowds.

The next morning, I went to the temple again. Amma was sitting in a room, and there was a queue of 10 – 15 people waiting for darshan. I did not even know what darshan was. Ravi-chettan urged me to join the queue. Though I hesitated initially, I eventually joined the line.

When I reached Amma, she hugged me and whispered a mantra in my ears. Some change took place within me. I felt an inexplicable closeness to her. The thought came to me that I must go to Amritapuri. Without waiting for Ravi-chettan to take me, one day, I set out alone for the ashram. When I reached Oachira, I asked an old man how to get to the ashram. He said he was going there, too, and we traveled to the ashram together.

When we reached the ashram, he showed me where Amma was. She was giving darshan in a small hut. Not knowing what to do, I stood outside as there were quite a few people inside. By the time I went in, it was time for bhajans. After that, I went for Devi Bhava darshan. Amma spoke to me with a lot of love and affection.

The next day, when I returned to Ernakulam, I learned that the ashram had bought some land in Kaloor. I became involved in the activities of the local ashram: construction of the ashram building, AYUDH, medical camps, archanas and bhajans in various houses... Amma's devotees soon began to replace my old friends.

I bought Amma's books and began reading them. I also read books on Sri Ramakrishna and books by his disciples. I became acquainted with Gopi-chettan, an ardent devotee of Sri Ramakrishna. I gained a lot of knowledge from him. Amma has graced his home twice.

Thereafter, for a long time, I kept visiting Amritapuri, until Amma gave me permission to join the ashram. I did not face much resistance from family members. However, close relatives and neighbors acted as if I had committed a serious crime! They did not know much about Amma then.

Afterwards, when the ashram grew and Amma became world famous, their opinions changed. Many of them started going to the Ernakulam Ashram to see Amma during her programs.

What kind of a devotee is dearest to the Lord? What qualities should he or she have? With what attitude should one worship God? The *Bhagavad Gita* addresses these questions in Chapter 12 (Bhakti Yoga).

The Lord says, "One who maintains equanimity and constantly sees and worships the Lord in all is dearest to me."

He elaborates on this:

> *samah shatrau ca mitre cha tatha manapamanayoh*
> *shitoshna sukhaduhkheshu samah sanga vivarjitah*
> *tulya ninda stutir mauni santushto yena kena cit*
> *aniketah sthiramatir bhaktiman me priyo narah*

> I like such a one who is the same to friend and foe; who does not lose composure in honor and dishonor; who retains equipoise in opposite experiences like cold and heat, and pleasure and pain; who is devoid of attachment to anything; to whom insult and praise are the same; who is silent; who is content with whatever comes to him by chance; who does not stick to any particular place; who has firmly established the intellect in the Self; and who is full of devotion. (*Bhagavad Gita*, 12.18 – 19)

In the devotee's eyes, there is neither friend nor foe, even though there might be people who hate the devotee. Isn't this true in

Amma's life also? There are people who are hostile to her. But that does not affect her.

We consider someone an enemy when he or she stands in the way of our needs. Likewise, we consider someone who is supportive a friend. A true devotee, however, is not worried about the body. He or she will neither discriminate between friend and foe nor be concerned about honor or dishonor, which pertain to the body alone.

Once, when Saint Eknath was returning from a bath in the Ganges, someone spat on him purposefully. Eknath patiently returned to the Ganges for another bath. When he emerged, the man spat again. This continued about 15 times. But Eknath had no complaints. He said, "I've been blessed with so many opportunities to bathe in the holy Ganges!"

Great souls like him demonstrate how to handle such situations in our own life. He was not offended when his body was insulted. But we find it difficult to understand this as we identify only with the body. As long as our awareness is confined to the body, we will not be able to accept honor and dishonor equally.

Lord Krishna says, "My devotee is equal in praise and insult." Generally, people enjoy being complimented. How happy we will be if Amma praised us! Conversely, when we are insulted, we react badly and out blood pressure will increase! Some people say, "I'm no Gandhi to forgive!" But, according to Lord Krishna, a true devotee has no sense of pride. He regards praise and insult equally, just as the tree gives shade to anyone, including the person who has come to cut it down.

I am reminded of a story associated with Sage Ashtavakra, a Self-realized soul. He was born with eight deformities on his body; hence the name: *ashta-vakra* (eight twists). Once, while still a boy, he went to King Janaka's court to take part in a debate among scholars. As soon as those assembled there saw him, they started laughing. Seeing this, Ashtavakra also started laughing, to their bemusement. The king asked him, "I can understand why the others are laughing. But why are you laughing?"

Ashtavakra replied, "I don't see any scholar here, only leather workers. They laugh, seeing the imperfections of my body. This shows that they do not behold the Self within me. If a pot breaks, the space within it doesn't. It is omnipresent, unattached to the pot, and devoid of attributes. My body is bent but I am not the body. I am the Self. These ignoramuses do not realize that."

Hearing his words, the scholars felt ashamed. Ashtavakra was not only unperturbed by insult, he had also corrected the scholars' misconceptions.

Just as a mountain remains unmoving whether the wind blows from the south or north, a true devotee remains indifferent to pleasure and pain. He regards everything as God's play. But in our case, we want everything to happen the way we like it though we do not know what is truly good for us.

Though life is an admixture of good times and bad times, happiness and sorrow, we do not acknowledge it. Some people think that they will turn to God in good times. What we ought to do instead is to think of God so as to make even our bad times good.

What is the cause of misery? Infatuation with objects. However, merely renouncing objects is not going to help us to be happy; we should give up our infatuation for them. If we can do so, even if we live amidst worldly objects, they will not affect us. King Janaka was a perfect example of such inner detachment.

Lord Krishna says as much:

apuryamanam achalapratishtam samudramapah pravishanti yadvat
tadvat kamayam pravishanti sarve sa shantimapnoti na kamakami

Just as the ocean remains unaffected even if waters enter it from all sides, one who remains unmoved by the swirl of sensory objects around him attains peace; one who tries to fulfill his desires will not. (*Bhagavad Gita*, 2.70)

Another quality of a true devotee is silence. This does not mean outer silence. Even if we do not talk, the chatter of the mind can still continue. A few years ago, a brahmachari was observing a vow of silence. He was supervising workers who had come to paint Amma's room. Amma was abroad at that time. This brahmachari started gesturing to the workers to shift some of the furniture in the room. Seeing this, one worker commented, "What a handsome man. Alas, he's dumb!" Another worker replied, "Don't worry. He's living here in the ashram. Amma will take care of him." Hearing this, the brahmachari lost his cool and said, "I'm not dumb!" So much for his silence!

The *Bhagavad Gita* defines austerity of the mind as follows:

manah prasadah saumyatvam maunam-atma-vinigrahah...

Serenity of mind, gentleness, silence and self-control... (16.17)

A true devotee is continuously contemplating God. He sees God everywhere because he perceives all that is sentient and insentient as forms of God. He is, therefore, a *sthita-prajna*, one whose awareness is firmly established in Self-realization. His mind does not waver.

Amma says that it is difficult to get established in wisdom without devotion. Quicklime alone is not enough to make cement; mortar must be added as well. Similarly, knowledge must blend with love. The vision of Truth is the experience that one is not the body but the Self or soul within. It is the understanding that only the body perishes, not the indwelling self. In the *Bhagavad Gita*, Lord Krishna compares the decaying body to soiled clothes. Amma uses the analogy of a light bulb. Only the bulb becomes impaired; the electric current remains.

It is said that man's greatest fear is that of death. There is only one way to dispel this fear: through *satsang*, i.e. companionship with Truth. This refers to the company of people established in Truth. Through satsang, *bhaya* (fear) gives way to *abhaya* (fearlessness). Abhaya also means refuge, i.e. taking refuge in God or the Guru.

A true devotee who is completely surrendered to God does not care about whether he is in heaven or hell. He is ever immersed in inner bliss. He is ever happy, irrespective of what food he gets to eat, what clothes he wears or where he sleeps. He remains satisfied, no matter what. In contrast, most people complain, "Not enough, not enough!" They always have complaints and grievances. Happiness eludes such people.

A man was going for a walk early in the morning. His wife prepared a hard-boiled egg for him. Seeing it, he said, "I would have preferred an omelet." The next morning, his wife prepared an omelet for him. Seeing it, the man said, "The hard-boiled egg was better." On the third day, the wife prepared both a hard-boiled egg and an omelet so that he could choose. Seeing this, he complained, "You fried the egg that was meant to be boiled and boiled the one meant to be fried!"

A true devotee has a pure mind and exclusive devotion to the Lord. Many years ago, I saw an unusual scene: Amma wearing a shirt while giving darshan. An old man was sitting near her. Upon inquiring, I learned that he was a farmer from a village near Erode in Tamil Nadu. An ardent devotee of Amma, he had the habit of offering whatever he received to Amma first. He would place it in his puja room first and use it only afterwards.

One day, his nephew had gifted him two shirts. Instantly, it occurred to him to offer them to Amma. As usual, he placed both shirts in his puja room. Thereafter, when he went to see Amma, he wore one of them. During darshan, he offered the other shirt to Amma. Amma asked him, "Son, to whom shall I give this?"

He said, "That's up to you, Amma."

Amma unfolded the shirt, put it on, and continued giving darshan. She spoke about his pure attitude to those around her. Thoughts like, "Amma is a woman who wears saris only and not shirts" did not occur to him. He just wished to offer it to Amma.

The Lord says,

ye tu dharmyamritamidam yathoktam paryupasate
shraddadhana matparama bhaktaste'tiva me priyah

One who honors this immortal law, which I declared, who has faith in me, and who regards me as the supreme goal and is devoted to me exclusively, is exceedingly dear to me. (*Bhagavad Gita*, 12.20)

This verse indicates the two qualities of a true devotee: faith in the Guru's words, and devotion to her with the sole aim of attaining divinity.

The words of a Guru are like a lamp. A flame does not point in any particular direction but gives light in all directions equally.

We can use this light to move forward. Similarly, we can use the form of the Guru to help us move inward towards our true nature. One who does so is dear to the Lord.

Having this knowledge helps us to understand and assimilate devotion. Lord Krishna has enumerated the qualities of a devotee so that we can remember and practice each one. The more we practice them, the more the darkness of ignorance will be dispelled and the closer we will move towards perfection.

We must visualize these virtues and strive to cultivate them. If we fail to, we must pine and cry for them. We must offer ourselves wholeheartedly to this *sadhana* (spiritual practice). This is also devotion.

It is not enough to glorify God. We must obey him as well. In addition, we must become aware of our limitations. Then, with the Guru's grace, we can rise above them.

These virtues are natural to *mahatmas* (spiritually illumined souls). We can see all the virtues of a true devotee in Amma. She has no hatred or anger towards anyone. She is interested only in alleviating suffering, wherever she sees it. Amma's decisions are not dependent on the opinions or perceptions of others. Once she has decided upon something, she will forge ahead confidently and cheerfully.

Once, the brahmachari in charge of the *Amritakuteeram* (free housing) project asked Amma, "Why help all these people, who only find fault with whatever we do for them?"

Amma replied, "Amma does not serve others based on what people say or do. Amma serves because it is Amma's nature to do so." She is firmly established in dharma and rooted in the Truth.

She does everything without a sense of ego. She does not attach herself to anything. Amma runs so many institutions. Yet, she is not proprietorial.

Swamiji (Swami Amritaswarupananda) often says, "If you carefully observe Amma, you can study everything." For example, during darshan, Amma conducts meetings by the side, gives various instructions, chats with and consoles devotees who come for darshan. She is a consummate multi-tasker and does not regard any one of these tasks as insignificant.

How and where to perform sadhana? Many people imagine that the ideal location for sadhana would be a solitary retreat by a river, in a forest, or in the Himalayas, where we imagine we can remain in peaceful contemplation of God. Almost everyone who leads a spiritual life would have entertained such thoughts. Nothing wrong with that. Even Amma says, "When you learn how to drive, you must do so in a place that is deserted." Yet, the scriptures and spiritual masters declare that the best place for sadhana is in the Guru's presence.

We are blessed to be living with Amma. She is always with us, meditating with us, singing bhajans with us, preparing food for us and serving us, swimming with us, joking with us, taking us with her on tours… Probably no Guru in history has done all this.

Amma is so encouraging. If we are nervous about giving a talk, she caresses our back to calm us down, and laughs at our jokes to bolster our confidence. Amma adopts different bhavas that will help us grow spiritually.

Once, when a boy was returning home from school, it began raining. The boy kept his books inside his shirt so that they would not get wet. When he reached home, he saw his mother standing by the door, waiting for him. She said, "You're soaking wet! You might catch a fever. Son, you could've placed the books on your head to shelter yourself from the rain." She then took the books from him, kept them aside, and affectionately dried his head with a towel.

On another occasion, when it rained again, the boy remembered what his mother had said and used his books to cover his head. When he reached home, he saw his father standing at the door. The father scolded him for treating his school books so carelessly.

Who was correct, the father or the mother? Both were. To the mother, her child is paramount, and that is why she was so affectionate to him. The father also loves his son but he is equally concerned about how society will judge his actions. Hence, he affects more sternness than the mother.

In the Guru, we can see a harmonious blend of both these qualities. Recently, during meditation, Amma said, "Both discipline and compassion are necessary." In the *Lalita Sahasranama* (1,000 names of the Divine Mother), two of the mantras are *raga-svarupa-pashadhya* and *krodha-karankushojvala* (mantras 8 and 9). Amma draws us to her with the rope of love and then disciplines us with the goad of sternness.

Amma has spoken about rudraksha trees and expressed her desire to see them in the ashram. They say that the wishes of mahatmas are *sankalpas* (divine resolves). To my knowledge, rudraksha trees are not found in this region; they grow only in the Himalayan locales. But now, there are a few hundred rudraksha trees here.

In a sense, we are all different kinds of plants and Amma is a gardener. Hers is a difficult job. Some can be planted easily. Others need to be tended with more care and need a lot of manure. Whatever type of plant we may be, if we are ready to submit to the earth, Amma will groom us into mighty trees capable of giving shade and fruit. In other words, we have the opportunity here, in Amma's sacred presence, to scale spiritual heights.

But it is not enough just to dream of greatness. We must gradually overcome our weaknesses, step by step, through perseverance.

Through spiritual practice, we must cultivate all the qualities of a true devotee. To succeed, we need Amma's grace. May she bless us all so that our actions become wholehearted, wholesome and worshipful offerings worthy of the divine. ◌◌◌

3

Sacred Paradise

Swamini Amalamrita Prana

A young man went to an ashram to learn meditation. He followed the Guru's teachings, became his disciple, obeyed the rules of the ashram, took part in the chanting and pujas, sang bhajans, and did selfless service. But even after staying in the ashram for years, the Guru, who reveled in the bliss of meditation, did not share the secrets of meditation with him. The disciple became anxious.

Days passed. The disciple's restlessness became evident in his behaviour, but the Guru pretended he hadn't noticed. He spoke kindly and lovingly to the disciple. At times, he would ask the disciple to sit close to him and then speak about the greatness of meditation, but he did not teach him how to meditate. Unable to contain his frustration, the disciple finally asked his Guru, "I've been living with you for years, and yet, you have not taught me how to meditate. Why?"

The Guru merely smiled.

After a few days, the Guru and disciple set out for a walk one evening. There were stars glittering in the sky. The moon had risen. In the calm silence, they heard the chirping of a bird from afar. The Guru asked, "Did you hear that?" The disciple said yes.

The next evening, they went for a walk again. They heard the chirping again. The Guru asked, "Can you tell which bird is chirping so melodiously?"

The disciple listened carefully and said, "Yes, it's a cuckoo."

On the third day, they heard the cuckoo warbling again. The Guru asked, "Can you sense the sweetness behind the singing?" The disciple suddenly understood what meditation was all about. He lost himself in the beauty of nature and did not hear what the Guru said after that.

Beauty is an integral element of meditation. There is beauty in the chirping of a bird and in the serenity exuded by flowers. In the caresses of the breeze, one can feel waves of bliss.

Amma has time and again said that meditation is not something one does in a secluded room. Attending to each and every one of our daily activities with total focus is real meditation. This is also karma yoga. In the *Bhagavad Gita*, Lord Krishna says,

> *loke'smindvividha nishta pura prokta mayanagha*
> *jnanayogena sankhyanam karmayogena yoginam*

> O sinless one, as previously explained, there is a two-fold path in this world: the path of knowledge for the Sankhyas (those inclined towards contemplation), and the path of action of the Yogis (those inclined towards action). (3.3)

The Lord is referring to the two time-honored practices — contemplation and action — that lead to Self-realization. The outcome of an action is based not only on what is done but also on how it is done. Kuchela offered just a handful of rice flakes to Lord Krishna. Though of negligible value materially, it was priceless for the Lord, who discerned pure love and devotion in each flake.

How much is a petal or a leaf worth? Its value is immeasurable if offered to God with love and reverence. When Satyabhama placed her priceless jewels on one pan of the balancing scale and Krishna sat on the other side, the jewels did not outweigh him. But when Rukmini placed just one *tulasi* (basil) leaf on the pan, the scale tipped towards the leaf. Why? Because Rukmini's devotion was worth more than the Lord's weight in gold.

Suppose a scholar and a devotee bathe in the Ganges. The scholar would have cleansed his body, but the devotee would have cleansed his body and purified his mind as well. So, the outcome of any action varies according the attitude behind it.

Amma asks, "Will a Guru adore the one who simply follows his words to the letter, or one who carries out the task with discernment?" She says the latter is dearer. Knowledge and action are not two distinct entities. Performing an action with awareness and knowledge is karma yoga.

In 1985, when I was in junior college, Amma visited the Sarada Mandir in Kozhikode. That is where my family members and I saw Amma for the first time. All of us became devotees instantly. Seeing her aroused in me an interest in living with her for the rest of my life. No one in my family objected to my wanting to join the ashram, but they wanted me to complete my degree first. Amma also told me to finish my degree before joining. Finally, with her consent, I joined the ashram in 1990.

My first seva was in the ashram's printing press. In those days, I did not know why I had to do seva. It is important to have at least some idea about what we are doing and why we are doing it. Swami Jnanamritananda was in charge of the press then. Once, he became angry with us for doing our work carelessly, asked us to leave, and locked up the press. Instead of feeling chastened, we rejoiced because we could go to Amma. We all went to the hut and sat near her. Seeing us all together, she asked, "What happened? Don't you have any work in the press?"

We happily said, "Swami sent us out and locked the press." Amma called Swami. When she learnt what had happened,

Amma lovingly told us that when we act, we must do so with awareness. This will help us to purify our thoughts.

After this incident, Amma started to monitor our work closely. She made it clear that we should not get distracted even if Amma walked past the press. She helped us understand that seva was worship, and for this reason, we should be totally focused on the task at hand.

There were only a few people working in the press back then. On days when there was no darshan, Amma would join the ashram residents and devotees in cleaning the ashram premises, carrying loads of sand for ongoing construction work, and doing other seva activities. Seeing this, those of us working in the press would feel sad that we could not join Amma and envious of those who could. Amma, who knew our hearts, would make up for it by surprise visits to the press at night. Usually, our work would continue until 2 or 3 a.m. Whenever she visited, she would carry a flask containing coffee in one hand, and a few packets of snacks in the other hand. She would say, "Children, how can Amma sleep when you are working late at night without any rest? After returning to the room, Amma will read letters. I wanted to give you coffee and snacks before that." Amma would spend a lot of time with us before leaving. If we could not attend bhajans owing to the heavy workload, Amma would come to the press afterwards and sing bhajans with us. In this way, our seva became a celebration. Only much later did we realize that Amma was transforming our karma into karma yoga, work into worship.

At one time, Amma suddenly stopped coming to the press. At first, we thought she was busy. But when she did not come even after many days, we began to worry. Did we do our work carelessly? Did we go against her wishes? Did we harbor impure thoughts? While we were speculating on the reasons for her absence, Amma sent Swami Amritatmananda to us. He asked us if we were all doing archana unfailingly. He said, "Amma does not feel like coming to the press because she thinks that some of you are not doing archana at all."

It was true. For various reasons, some of us were not doing archana. This clearly revealed to us that Amma is not limited to her physical form. She is the all-pervading pure consciousness and is with us subtly. This experience convinced us of Amma's omniscience.

In the press, Vasanthi-chechi and I used to make printing plates. Before Amma's birthday, we would be very busy with the new book releases. Vasanthi-chechi and I would spend all our time making plates in the image processing room and then give the plates to the brahmacharis, who would work 24-hour shifts to finish printing the books before the birthday. Once, we found that we could not even see Amma for days on end and became sad. We found it hard to concentrate on work. Finally, we decided to make as many plates as necessary at one go so that we could see Amma. In this way, we managed to finish the work in time.

We heard that Amma had gone to the brahmacharinis' quarters. Just as we were about to go there, the brahmachari in charge of printing appeared in front of us and said, "The plate you gave us is damaged. We need another one. We cannot print with the plate you gave us." Hearing this, we became terribly disappointed. We felt that we should do the seva that Amma had assigned us to the best of our abilities and continued working for another 30 – 45 minutes before leaving. We were not sure if Amma had returned to her room. As luck would have it, she was still there. She had come to oversee the kitchen construction work and was in one of the rooms with the brahmacharinis when we arrived. We heard Amma's voice and laughter. As there was no space inside the room, we stood at the door. As soon as we reached, Amma got up to go. A battalion of brahmacharinis followed her. Hiding our sadness, we moved aside and pressed ourselves against the wall so that others could pass. While passing, Amma took my hand and pressed something into my palm, closed it, and walked on. When I went to the press, I saw that she had given me a little prasad. Throughout that day, I could smell Amma's lingering scent on my hand.

When our mind gets purer, we stop blaming others for mistakes and instead become aware of our own flaws. I am reminded of a story that Amma tells. A newlywed couple moved into their new apartment. Through the window, the young bride could see freshly washed clothes hanging on her neighbor's clothes line. She told her husband, "See that? Those clothes are not really clean. Perhaps the woman of the house doesn't know how to wash clothes properly." The husband remained silent.

Every day, the wife would pass the same comment, and the husband would not respond. After a few weeks, she told her husband, "Did you see that? That woman has finally learnt how to wash clothes. The clothes on the line today are spotless. I wonder who taught her how to do the laundry properly."

The husband said, "This morning, I cleaned our windows. It was because of the dirt and grime on our windows that you perceived their clothes as dirty."

If we try to do any work that Amma assigns us, as worship or with the attitude of being an instrument in God's hands, that action will be transformed. This attitude of surrender draws the Guru's grace, which will wash away the selfishness and egoism from our hearts. Over time, the mirror of our hearts will become clean. Then, we will be able to perceive only goodness in everything.

If we exercise our God-given faculties of awareness and discernment, we can serve the world and evolve spiritually. Amma made quite a few brahmacharinis obtain their Bachelor's and Master's degrees in Education and then assigned them the responsibility of taking charge of the Amrita Vidyalayam schools. Amma first sent me to Pulpally, where I served for several years. One day, Amma sent me to Karwar in Karnataka. As I do not know Kannada, this assignment came as a shock not only to me but to others as well. Nevertheless, I firmly believed that she would take care of everything.

I was reminded of an incident that took place in the ashram's swimming pool years ago. We were lining up to be pushed by Amma into the pool. When my turn came, I became scared and told Amma about it. She said, "Once you have learnt swimming, you won't forget it." Amma then pushed me into the water. Fortunately, I fell into the life ring placed in the water for that purpose. I didn't have to do anything. By moving my legs a little, I was able to make it to the shallow end of the pool. Amma's sending me to Pulpally and Karwar proved to be as effortless as this experience. I felt Amma's divine power acting within me. All I had to do was to be an instrument in her hands.

Let me share a story I heard. It was time to declare the final results in a school. The principal wanted to promote all the students, provided each one could prove his or her competency. Each student was to take on a project; those who could not complete it would be retained. However, the time given to finish the project was insufficient. The teacher started thinking of ways to promote all his students, all of whom were intelligent. An idea struck him. He drew a star on the board and asked the students to do likewise in their books. Walking around the class, he noticed that some students had drawn magnificent stars. Some stars were mediocre, and some were downright bad. The teacher whispered something into the ears of the students who could draw well. He also whispered something to those who could not draw well.

The headmaster came to evaluate the students. The teacher drew a star on the board and wrote: 'Fill in the blanks.' Each student was asked to come up and draw whatever they could on the board. When they finished, the headmaster saw a beautiful constellation on the board: there were stars in various shapes and a beautiful moon. There were also many dots. The headmaster asked the teacher what the dots were. The teacher said they were distant stars. The headmaster was impressed and told the teacher to promote all the students.

What had the teacher done? He told those who could draw well to draw the stars and the moon and the others to put a dot.

Isn't this what Amma, the universal protector, is also doing? We have all reached her after many births. In her boundless compassion, Amma has created various opportunities for us to serve and exhaust our karmic debts. Can't we make a dot at least? She says, "Children, simply do whatever you can. Just be; that's enough. Amma will take care of the rest."

If we make the best use of this opportunity, our lives will be truly blessed. May Amma bestow her grace on all. ☙

4

Those Eyes

Br. Rishi Chaitanya

Amma says, "The Guru is like a huge doorway through which the disciple can move forward on the spiritual path. To do so, the disciple should enter the heart of the Guru. The Guru is the noblest and most trusted friend, who awakens us to the reality that 'I am not this small entity; I am infinite, as pervasive as the sky. I am fullness itself.'"

What is this inner doorway? It is a great mystery. Something opens up inside that we previously had no access to, which we never even knew existed. This doorway is the inner Guru. It is through this opening inside that the disciple is able to glimpse and feel her true nature, which is also our true nature.

She says, "In the spiritual life, two meetings take place: the outer meeting of the Guru and the inner meeting of the Guru. We need to have encountered both meetings in order to move forward in spiritual life."

I first met Amma in 1996 in San Ramon, California. I was 18 years old. Amma was giving Devi Bhava darshan. I made my way up the stairs to the balcony, and sat above where Amma was giving darshan, looked around and took in the scene. The atmosphere was vibrant and beautiful. One by one, people of different ages, backgrounds and nationalities went to Amma to be embraced. Captivating as that scene was, what was more splendid was the light that seemed to surround Amma. It wasn't anything supernatural. I somehow *felt* it was there.

After watching Amma for a long time, I closed my eyes and felt within myself the same light as the most soothing and comforting motherly presence. That presence was so alive and new, yet utterly familiar. It seemed like a presence that had been dormant in my life for as long as I can remember. I spent that whole night on the balcony, watching Amma with open eyes, and then closing my eyes and talking to and being held by that wonderful presence.

As nobody had told us to stay until the end of Devi Bhava, my friends and I left early. While driving out of the ashram, our car slid down an embankment and into a ditch. We spent half an hour trying to get the car out. At one point, while my friends were still trying, I took a break. I climbed up to the road and sat on the curb.

Suddenly, a Lexus driving down from the temple slowly pulled up and stopped in front of me. Someone rolled down the window. It was Amma! Her eyes were like two shining suns. We looked at each other. My jaw dropped open and I said, "Amma?" She gave me a big smile and the car drove off.

I didn't see Amma for many months after that, but those eyes became my refuge. Even when I closed my eyes and visualized them, something would open up within me. Every thought of her eyes seemed to open an inner doorway for me.

Later I learnt from Amma that when we internalize our experiences with the Guru—be it a darshan, a look, a smile, a word, the touch of Amma's cheek, or the feel of her hand—they become an opening to the peace of our true self. It was by this technique alone—internalizing and reliving their experiences with Lord Krishna—that the *gopis* (milkmaids) of Vrindavan were able to realize God after the Lord left Vrindavan. Even now, I still visualize Amma's eyes during meditation; that technique remains ever fresh.

Lord Krishna says,

yo mam pashyati sarvatra sarvam ca mayi pashyati
tasyaham na pranashyami sa ca me na pranashyati

One who sees me everywhere and everything in me never
loses sight of me; nor do I lose sight of him. (*Bhagavad
Gita*, 6.30)

This is my favorite verse in the whole *Gita* because it shows the
peak of divine love, where the devotee becomes one with God.
For many people, before meeting Amma, God was just a word.
But after meeting her, God became an experience. This is Amma's
greatest miracle: awakening that love in each one of us. That love is
no different from God or our true self. Little by little, we begin to
feel that love behind everything. Amma has said that there is only
one way to enter the doorway to God, and that is through love.

When I first met Amma, I wondered if it was really possible
to have such an intimate relationship with God, as indicated by
this verse from the *Gita*. Could one experience a closeness to the
divine that was just as real as an intimate human relationship?

When I came to India, I found that this verse was really true.
I was still a teenager when I left my family and made the journey
to Amritapuri in 1997. I had never been out of the US before.
Although I had a spiritual hunger, still, being so far away from
everything familiar to me wasn't easy.

At that time, there were not many amenities in the ashram. I
found it hard to fit in and get used to life around Amma and in
the ashram. To be honest, I often felt, "I don't know if I can do
it. Maybe, I better go home..."

It was then that I became acquainted with one of the greatest
secrets of this ashram: the ocean. It changed my life here forever.
Over the next few years, she became my closest companion. I
have poured my heart out to her so many times. I used to feel

that no matter how bad a day I had, whenever I went there, she would rush to greet me, and I would lie in her lap and tell her all that was on my mind. This became for me more powerful than praying in any temple or before any deity.

I soon learnt that I wasn't the only one who had this relationship with the ocean. At that time, I used to live in the small dormitory below Amma's room. I used to sleep next to the window. Many times at night, I used to hear Amma sneak out. She would go to the seashore to meditate, pray, talk to and sing to the Divine Mother in the form of the ocean. Mother Ocean was Amma's refuge when she was growing up. It was to her that Amma used to pour her heart out when no one else understood her.

Once, when it was past midnight, someone came to our dormitory and said, "Amma's calling you to the beach!" We went there and sat around Amma, who sang bhajans and meditated in the dark for a long time. Then Amma said, "Okay, children. Go back to bed. Amma will stay here a while longer." She did not allow even her attendant, Bri. Lakshmi (now Swamini Srilakshmi Prana), to stay with her. Amma said, "I have so many things to tell the ocean. She may not listen if you're here."

I remember looking at Amma as I walked back. Her eyes were locked on the horizon. Although I had read about Amma's sadhana days, it was on that night that I really felt her relationship with the Divine Mother. I remember thinking, "This is why I've come here. This is what I want to have. I want to be able to pour out my heart to that inner presence, and have that kind of intimate relationship with God."

Amma says that each one of us has this inner relationship, but we have overlooked it for so long that we have lost touch with it. Seeing Amma communing with and demonstrating her great love for God right before my eyes was a tremendous experience. It is from her that we can learn how to pray to and commune with that source of love within. From her, we can learn to perceive the living presence behind forms of nature such as the ocean, trees and the sky. These are things you cannot learn from books. You can only learn them by being in the presence of a realized master.

But the way this relationship with the Guru unfolds in each of our lives is different and unique. This is what makes it so special and sacred.

About 10 years ago, while traveling with Amma in the US, I invited a friend of mine to the Los Angeles program. He asked me a lot of questions and was looking forward to meeting Amma. We met at the program and talked for a while. I got him a token before the start of the Devi Puja. When Devi Bhava started, I became busy with my seva and we did not see each other for the rest of the night.

The next day, I called him on the phone and asked him, "How was your night? How was darshan? Did you meet Amma? Tell me all about it."

"Well," he said, "After we parted, I didn't even know where to go. It was so crowded and loud, and people everywhere were bumping into each other. Finally, I made it to the darshan line. People kept telling me to move and then to wait. It was so confusing, and honestly, I was a little irritated. Just before I reached the stage, someone asked me, 'Do you want a mantra?' I said, 'No, I don't.' I don't even know what a mantra is!

"Finally, I got to the stage, and before I knew it, someone was turning me this way and that way. When I got close to Amma, someone got me to kneel. Someone else removed my glasses. Someone started wiping my face with a cloth... I was getting disoriented. When I was finally kneeling just in front of Amma, someone suddenly stuck his head right in front of me and asked, 'What's your native tongue?'

"'My native what? Tongue???'

"While I was thinking about my tongue, Amma grabbed me and started mumbling something in my ear. I was wondering, 'What's she saying? Is it English?' I then got pulled backwards, turned and released.

"I thought, let me just find a place to sit on the stage and take in whatever happened... but there was no place. So, I left the stage and wandered around for a while. The crowds, the people, the music... I finally just got fed up and went back home!"

I was taken aback. I said, "I'm so sorry. I wasn't expecting that at all."

He said, "But you know, when I woke up this morning, the oddest thing happened. I just started crying, and I felt a kind of peace inside that I had never felt before..."

After a long pause, he quietly said, "I just can't get the thought of her out of my mind. I want to go to the next program!"

He did. He flew all the way there, and spent the next two days sitting in the hall, watching Amma, meditating, praying and connecting to that deeper part of himself that he was just starting to access.

This is how it is for many of us: when the outer meeting of the Guru leads to the inner meeting with her, our lives change forever.

This is not to say that being with the Guru is easy. When I first met Amma and started spending time with her, it was wonderful. But at the same time, something unexpected entered my life — pain. I was totally unprepared for it. Being with the Guru has been more painful than I could ever have imagined. As the yearning to get closer to Amma becomes stronger, we start to see everything — our weakness, ego, desires and *vasanas* (latent tendencies) — that stands between us and our goal. It can be overwhelming and painful because though we know what we want, we are not able to get it. We realize we need help.

This is where the Guru comes in. She is the embodiment of God's love within us, and she will help us overcome those obstacles. But it is not an easy task.

Once we were sitting with Amma in a place of natural beauty. She looked at all of us and said, "You all look like beautiful flowers. But Amma's job is to look for the worms in each one of these flowers and wait for the right moment to remove them!" This 'worm removal' can be painful.

Many years ago, we were staying in a devotee's house during a tour. In the morning, we got ready for the program and rushed out of the house, leaving it in a mess. Late that night, Amma told our host, "Amma wants to stay in your house tonight!"

At first, she was thrilled, and then she panicked! The program was almost over and nothing was ready. The house was a mess. All of us who were staying there left the program early, jumped into our cars, and raced back to the house. When we got there, we gathered the sleeping bags, dirty clothes, wet laundry, towels, plates, and dumped them all into one of the bedrooms. As we were doing this, the doorbell rang. Thinking that other devotees had come to help, the host opened the door; Amma was standing there with the swamis! In her panic, she slammed the door in their faces, and yelled, "Amma's here!"

We ran, made arrangements for the *pada puja* (ceremonial washing of Amma's feet), and then opened the door. Amma walked in and the pada puja began.

In the meantime, the husband was still upstairs, wildly shoving things into the room. Hearing the arati bell, he came dashing down so fast that he fell right in front of Amma!

After the puja, Amma went into the kitchen, cracked jokes, gave prasad to everyone, and went upstairs to her room. A room had been specially prepared for Amma. It was kept meticulously clean all year and was revered as the 'Guru's room.' But when

Amma went up, to the absolute horror of the hosts, she took a sharp left, went straight into the bedroom with all the mess, and shut the door. That is where Amma stayed!

We can put on a mask and fool everyone but the Guru. She goes right to where the dirt is, where our weakness and shortcomings are. And that is where she stays, reflecting what we are, like a mirror. But the Guru does this purely out of love. Her only desire is to bridge the gap between us and God, and to help us recognize and remove those obstacles. This can be painful, overwhelming and intense. Amma says that the Guru may even create situations to make us aware of our ego.

Our efforts can take us to a certain point, perhaps to the threshold. But to go deeper in our meditation, to pass that doorway or to enter the heart of the Guru, our efforts will not suffice. When I began to see all my weakness, desires and negativities coming up again and again, I felt totally overwhelmed and told Amma about it. She said, "You must learn to face your weaknesses and negativities squarely, not with fear but with love, holding on to the Guru's hand."

Anyone can learn to do spiritual practices. But letting go of the ego and being an open book before the Master takes tremendous courage.

There is a deep and integral bond between God, ourselves and the Guru. When we draw closer to the Guru, and open up to her completely, we will find those barriers to this bond dissolving in a mysterious way. The relationship with the Guru is the sweetest; it is also the most difficult.

The following incident took place about 20 years ago in Chennai during a Brahmasthanam program. It was late at night, around 2 a.m., and I was washing pots. Someone ran to me and said, "Amma is calling you for darshan!" As I did not have time to change, I quickly ran. Darshan was just about over. I reached

Amma. She didn't say anything. She just held me by my shoulders and brought her face close to mine until we were nose to nose. Her eyes were brilliant. They were gazing into my eyes with so much love that I felt as if I were falling into those endlessly deep eyes...

And then, it was over. She let me go, and I walked away in a daze. But that experience of Amma looking into my eyes like that went so deep inside me that it has become a part of me. I just have to think of it and I will feel it.

There was a Christian saint known as Teresa of Avila. Once, a nun asked her, "Sister, how do you meditate? How do you commune with Jesus within?"

She said, "It's very simple. I look at him and he looks at me."

There are no words, just a deep feeling, a flow, love... And if we take that thought and drop it, all that remains is a stillness, oneness, peace.

When we internalize all our experiences with the Guru—be it a look, a smile, a word, the touch of Amma's cheek, or the feel of her hand—they become an opening to the peace of our true self.

May we always feel Amma's divine eyes peering at us from behind all of nature—the sky, the flowers, the ocean... May we hold on tightly to the Guru's hand as we go through difficult times when she cleans our 'dirty rooms.' Let us never forget that no matter where we are, what we have to go through, or how many times we fall down, we are never alone. Know that she never—not even for a moment—loses sight of us. ౿౿౿

5

Contentment
Bri. Nirlepamrita Chaitanya

In 1992, while studying in the Calicut University, my roommate told me about Amma and about her experiences with Amma. Her accounts were so riveting that I began thinking about Amma. That night, I dreamt that I had her darshan. I could feel her love and even got a whiff of her fragrance.

The next day, I saw a newspaper advertisement announcing 'Amma in Calicut.' The paper carried a photo of Amma, whom I recognized from my dream the night before. My urge to meet Amma began to grow.

At 7 a.m. the next morning, I went to the venue of Amma's program and joined the darshan line. At 4 p.m., I was still in the queue. As I had to be back in the hostel before 6 p.m., I decided to leave. As I was nearing the gate, a man came running to me, saying that Amma was calling me. I thought it was a case of mistaken identity. How could she possibly be calling me when we had not even met? I ignored him and started walking away. The man blocked my way and said, "I must take you to Amma. It was she who told me to take you to her."

That is how I first went to Amma. When she saw me, she behaved as if she had known me for a long time. Hugging me, Amma said, "How can you leave without getting darshan?" It was the same darshan I had in my dream! That day, I realized that even though I had everything, there was a big emptiness in my life. Deep in my heart, I had been craving something. I did not know what that was until this darshan: it was the bond with a Satguru.

In 1996, Amma let me join the ashram. Before that, I had been living in the Sarada Math. I loved the ambience of spiritual discipline there, and the residents of that ashram were very loving to me. When I started living in Amritapuri, I realized how different life is in the presence of a divine incarnation. Amma is Parashakti, the Almighty. She is Goddess Bhavatarini, whom Sri Ramakrishna worshipped and who incarnated as Amma.

Amma provides direct guidance to each aspirant here. All that a seeker needs is available here: archana, scriptural and Sanskrit classes, meditation, yoga classes, chanting, puja, satsangs, bhajans... How can one not be happy here? If one cannot be happy here, where else can one be happy?

Lord Krishna says,

yadrccha-labha-santushto dvandatito-vimatsarah
samah siddhavasiddhau ca krtvapi na nibadhyate

He who is content with whatever comes to him without effort, who has overcome all dualities and envy, who is even-minded in success and failure, even if he acts, his actions will not bind. (*Bhagavad Gita*, 4.22)

Amma tells us the same thing: that, like other decisions, happiness is also a decision.

A karma yogi is satisfied with whatever comes his way. He strives to free himself from jealousy and rivalry, and from dualities such as joy and sorrow, success and failure, and praise and contempt. He does his duty dispassionately, and remains even-minded in victory and defeat.

Amma tells the story of an elderly king who wanted to find a successor to the throne. He did not have children. In such cases, the practice in the kingdom was to send a royal elephant out with a garland in its trunk. The person it garlanded would be the next ruler.

The elephant garlanded a beggar, who tried to run away, not knowing what was happening. Soldiers caught him, took him to the palace, and told him that he was going to be the next king. In due course, the old king died and the erstwhile beggar was crowned. After a few years on the throne, he wanted to re-experience his old life. Putting on tattered rags, he went out.

Some people gave him alms. Some threw food into his begging bowl. A few shooed him away. He recalled how he had reacted to each of these situations in his earlier life. He used to be elated when he received a lot of food or money. If he received nothing or was shouted at, he used to feel sad and hurt. Now, knowing that he was a king, with the royal treasury at his disposal, he was moved by neither generosity nor miserliness. He was able to accept whatever he received with equanimity.

Mahatmas (spiritually illumined souls) are like that. They are *purna* (whole, perfect). Nothing external affects them. We see this perfect contentment and equanimity in Amma all the time. She sees her own *svarupa* (true nature), which is pure consciousness, in others, too.

Most people have a tendency to compare themselves with others. When we think we are doing better than others, we become proud. When they have done better than us, we feel sad and jealous. A *jnani* (knower of the Truth) knows that we are all parts of a whole, and is therefore not affected by pride or jealousy. His mind is always calm and steady. He does his duties for the welfare of the world. He acts as if he were an instrument in the hands of God, and so, lacks the sense of being a doer. His actions are not prompted by *vasanas* (latent tendencies) and do not create new vasanas. His actions are a blessing to the world.

These qualities are inborn in Amma. It is difficult to understand or evaluate her actions. If we observe how she receives devotees, we can intuit her total lack of egoism. Amma becomes totally identified with the happiness or sorrow of each person who comes to her; the subject and object merge into the non-dual one.

Some people ask what one gets from meeting Amma. Let me recount an incident I witnessed during darshan. A young man was brought in a wheelchair to Amma. With much distress, he described to Amma how he had been suffering from a serious disease for the last decade. Amma embraced him and also cried. When his darshan ended, the man seemed to have received a new lease on life. An unknown peace and satisfaction lit up his face. He said, "My friends and relatives deserted me a long time ago. But now I have a mother! Even if I do not recover from the disease, I don't mind because I have finally met someone who shares my pain. But from now on, I will not be sad, because if I cry, my Amma will also cry."

In her presence, we forget ourselves and the world, and reach a state wherein we do not need anything, i.e. we are content. This is the biggest gain one could have.

The next person who went for darshan had happy news. Amma shared his joy whole-heartedly. He, too, gained total satisfaction.

How is Amma able to satisfy everyone? All her actions arise from a sense of completeness. She is ever content. She does not depend on anything external for her contentment. Amma is helping us turn within and become self-reliant so that we stop leaning on outer objects for our happiness.

In 2006, Amma told me to go to the Kannur Amrita Vidyalayam. She added, "I'm going to make you live there alone."

I tried my best to wriggle out of it, saying, "Amma, please don't send me there alone. I don't know anything. What can I do there on my own?"

But Amma did not relent. She said, "Just be there. I will do everything."

How can we have doubts or fears when we become an instrument in Amma's hands? When we depend fully on her, surrender becomes natural. She was also teaching me that the mind should not cave in when it encounters difficult situations. Instead, we should accept them as God's or the Guru's will, and strive to move forward.

Once, a brahmachari asked Amma, "What do we do when others consider our patience a weakness?"

Amma replied, "Son, how does it matter to you if others consider you weak? Doesn't your question mean that you expect recognition from others? You have come to the spiritual path to realize your Self. Why should you worry about what others think of you?"

Through her response, Amma is trying to make us cultivate an attitude of accepting all experiences patiently, and to develop equanimity in the face of both praise and scorn.

One New Year's Eve, Amma came to the hall. After the prayer, when she started distributing prasad, people rushed to her and surrounded her. I tried moving towards her to get the prasad, but could not, owing to the rush. Questions arose in my mind. How can I navigate my way through this thick crowd? If I wait for some more time, will I get the prasad? What if I don't receive any prasad? Then, a contrary thought came to me. Isn't everything we receive here Amma's prasad? If so, let me be patient and content.

Suddenly, Amma turned and so did the crowd around her. I do not know what happened, but the next moment, I found Amma in front of me. She was distributing the prasad with her right hand.

I stood dazed and even forgot to extend my hand. With her left hand, Amma took my right hand and put some prasad into it. She even pressed my fingers on the prasad so that it would not fall out of my palm. A moment later, she moved away, distributing prasad to others. The crowd also moved away along with her.

I was totally stunned. I could not believe what had happened. I had not moved a single step from where I had been standing, and yet I had received the prasad in my hands. How? When I tried to imagine everything as God's will, Amma's prasad had reached my hands! We may not always get such a mind, but I try to contemplate on this experience often.

Discontentment can be dangerous, as the following story reveals. A fisherman found a large and beautiful pearl. But there was a scratch on it. He thought that if he removed the blemish, it would become the most beautiful pearl in the world. He started filing the pearl's surface to remove the stain, but it did not disappear. The fisherman continued filing it vigorously until the whole pearl was eventually ground to powder. The scratch on the pearl disappeared; but, so, too, the pearl!

Nothing in creation is perfect. If the fisherman had kept that invaluable pearl as it was, he would not have lost it. However, his dissatisfaction and ambition caused him to destroy the treasure.

Once, I went to Udupi for a school inspection, where I was given a gift. When I returned, I unwrapped the gift. It was a beautiful silver vessel! The moment I saw it, I decided to give it to Amma, who was abroad then. When she returned, I went with the gift for Amma's darshan. When I was near Amma, I felt a little embarrassed about giving her the vessel. So, I tried to slowly push it under her chair without her noticing it.

Suddenly, someone snatched it from my hands. It was Amma! Raising it with her left hand, she asked, "Where did you get this?"

I said, "Amma, I received it as a gift when I went to a school in Udupi for an inspection."

"You mean to say that you accepted a bribe?" demanded Amma.

I tried to make Amma understand that it was not a bribe at all. I gave the example of how the ashram gives books to guests as gifts.

As if she had not heard what I said, Amma said, "So, you accepted a bribe." She then raised the gift and showed it to everyone, saying, "Our children have been recognized by the CBSE (Central Board of Secondary Education). They are being invited to inspect schools."

Then Amma told me, "Daughter, whenever you go for inspections to schools, do not accept any gift. If you are offered a gift, return it, saying that you have accepted it, but let it remain in that school."

I agreed. As I was getting up, I told Amma that I could not tell her about my inspection earlier as she was not in India then. Amma said that she knew about it as she had read my letter.

What did Amma mean? I had not given her any letter. Later, after I returned to Kannur, I realized what had happened. As I stay alone in the school, as a matter of self-discipline, I used to write letters to Amma whenever I had to go out, and would keep these letters in a diary. I had done so before going to Udupi.

Amma's words revealed to me that she knows all that I do and think. This experience inspired me to continue writing to Amma.

Since then, whenever I go for school inspections, I do exactly what Amma told me to do with gifts. My hosts would look surprised, but I feel a deep satisfaction carrying out Amma's instructions.

Each one of our thoughts pass through Amma. Knowing this, let us try to tune ourselves more deeply to Amma. This should be a constant endeavor. If we can sustain this effort, every moment in life will become a precious experience. May Amma bless us all with an attitude of acceptance and surrender. ৩৯৯

6

Fear and Love

Br. Satvamrita Chaitanya

Before I met Amma, I was a rocker. I wore all black — black jeans and black T-shirt. My hair reached halfway down my back. I was in the ninth grade and everyone in my school thought I was weird. After I met Amma, I returned to school in all white — white *dhoti*, white T-shirt and a clean-shaven head. Everyone in my school thought I was weird. But I didn't care. I was in love. And when you're in love, your whole perspective changes.

The story of the human race can be seen as a tussle between fear and love, between manipulating our surroundings or living in harmony with them.

> The story of the human race is a story of survival,
> from darkness to light, from trial to trial,
> of biological impulses and moral complexities,
> except for the ones brave enough to make sense of these.
> It's the story of a mother's sacrifice and her children's
> greed, as they ravage a planet without thought or
> compassion,
> until creation reminds them, they are not alone,
> that this beautiful planet is not only their home.

This is our story. We have reached impressive technological heights but nature has shown that, in the end, she will outlast us. We are fragile creatures, ready to break at the slightest change in the elements. This sudden awareness of our fragility has plunged the world into fear. Amma has said, "Without faith, we are full of fear. Fear cripples the body and mind, paralyzing us, whereas faith opens our hearts and leads us to love."

Instead of wanting to live in harmony with nature, we often choose to exploit it for our own benefits. The only time we turn to God is when fear grips us, when we realize that we are not in control. As soon as the situation is resolved and the fear leaves us, we immediately return to the lifestyle that caused the problems in the first place.

People all over the world are intensely agitated because of the coronavirus pandemic. But COVID-19 is our story, the story of the human race. It is a tale of fear versus love. It has put death front and center, forcing the whole world to pause and ask: "What is important to us? What are our core values? Why are we even here?"

Amma has been warning us for years about the impending changes in nature, and has shown us the way ahead. Every single day, Amma leads us in the White Flowers of Peace meditation, saying, "In today's world, the human mind and nature are in an agitated state. Only divine grace can help us bring peace into our hearts and to our planet."

As humans, we seem to have an innate drive to master both nature and each other but not ourselves. But spirituality teaches that 'isha vasyam idam sarvam'—everything is God. The only way forward in a world gripped by fear and overwhelmed by the ego is to maintain this awareness. To understand what it means to live with this attitude, we need only watch how Amma flows through this world, in harmony with the seeming chaos around her.

When she walks into a room, it is not with the intention of selling something. When politicians, business leaders, religious leaders or even humanitarians and activists walk into a room, they all want to sell something; they all need our support. But Amma doesn't want anything from us. All she wants to do is uplift us. And she doesn't need anything for that. She doesn't even need to say or do anything. All she has to do is walk into the room. By lifting the level of our consciousness, we become aware of our selfish motives. At that level, love always wins. Fear has no place where love has taken over.

You can see this even when Amma walks into a place where no one knows her. Take an airport, for example. She may be accompanied by swamis and swaminis, brahmacharis and brahmacharinis, devotees and children, all with big smiles, and standing tall in their beautiful colors; all proud to be walking with Amma. But anyone watching knows where the action is. Even if they have never heard of or seen Amma before, they know. It's the short, unassuming one in the plain white dress. They don't know who or what she is but they all know: it's her. And how do they express that? They put their hands on their chest, laugh or cry when they see her. Why? Even though their minds don't know it, their hearts do. It's love. She is vibrating with that divine love, and people can't help but respond to that. Like the white petals of peace falling from the sky, she envelopes everyone around her in the safe, blissful space in which she exists; that place where we all feel at home.

Those who encounter this love receive it in their own way. Everyone has a personal love filter. Amma is like the Advaita (non-dual) philosophy—there is only One, but people imagine her in as many ways as there are imaginations. But because it's being given and received with love, it will always uplift. Love can only elevate, even when misunderstood.

I have my own experience with this. When I was 15, I heard Amma's satsang for the very first time. There was one point that she made that has stayed with me for the last few decades. The only problem was, initially, I misunderstood the point completely. Amma said something like, "Only humans have the power of discrimination. Dogs don't discriminate." What Amma meant was that only humans have the power to discriminate between right and wrong, real and unreal, and that they can use this power to propel them on the path towards God-realization. But as a 15-year-old American boy born to a black father and a white mother, making me a minority in the US, I could only think of negative discrimination: discriminating against someone on the basis of race, religion or social standing. So, I thought, how profound this teaching is. A dog does not discriminate. No matter how its master acts—whether he beats it or cuddles it, feeds it or doesn't feed it, or just ignores it—the dog always runs to the master with love. I thought, dogs are great and humans are stupid. I was hooked! Amma was a civil rights leader! Yes, Amma is a civil rights leader, but I was missing the point.

Even the dog in my story chose love over fear. What about us?

Once I asked Amma a question merely to engage her in conversation. Many of you know that unless you are ready for anything, this is probably not the best idea. To make it worse, I had been thinking of what question Amma would like to hear from me to get me into her good books, as if we could be in the bad books of someone whose very life is dedicated to serving everyone. To provide a context for my question, let me share a little bit of history.

I moved from Amma's San Ramon Ashram to Amritapuri in 1994. I had been begging Amma for years to let me come but she would always say, "Not yet. Finish school." But finally, in the summer of '94, she said, "Okay, you try." I didn't know enough at the time to understand that this meant, "Okay, you've been warned!" It didn't go quite as planned.

Coming from the San Ramon Ashram, where I was a big fish in a small pond, I was not ready to be a tiny tadpole in the ocean of Amritapuri. I had my whole future planned out. I was going to be Amma's harmonium player in a few short weeks. I was going to meditate like a saint the rest of the time. And Amma was going to give me so much attention and sing my praises to everyone because I was her favorite. Things didn't work out that way. My master plan wasn't the Master's plan.

Many of us join the ashram and forget who the Guru is. We might want to change things according to our own likes and dislikes. We might try to import our own ideas of spirituality, or what devotees should or shouldn't be doing. We might want to implement our own business ideas, or sway Amma to our own humanitarian causes. Or we might try and drag our worldly logic into spiritual matters. But struggle as we may, there can be only one Guru.

After a year of not being able to walk along the path that Amma had laid out before me in Amritapuri, I left. I locked up my hut in the middle of the night and fled to America. As Amma would later put it, I came to grow spiritually but all I did was find fault with everything. I ran back to San Ramon, and blamed my leaving on the ashram, when in truth, I was just not ready to take the blows to my ego, which were plunging me into fear and mental agitation.

Actually, I didn't return to the San Ramon ashram immediately. I first went to my mother's house for a month. The US Tour was a month away. That year, the Seattle retreat was on an island about two hours away from the city. I decided to skip the retreat and wait until Amma came for the Seattle programs to face the music. When my mother went for darshan at the retreat, Amma started talking about me, saying that she feels very sad when she sees someone who, lacking knowledge about spirituality, has no idea what is going on. My mom was defensive for my sake. She disagreed, saying that I was still meditating and singing bhajans. Amma shook her head and said, "If he's still meditating, then he needs a Guru, and if he wants one, then he better get here now!"

So, I went. When I arrived at the retreat, Amma just filled me with love, and in her light, I saw my own mistakes. I saw the mess that I had allowed my fear of the unknown to create in my life.

After the tour, I moved back to the San Ramon Ashram, intent on doing things on Amma's time. She told me to get a job outside, do ashram work, and finish school. And that's what I did.

That brings me back to the question that I was going to ask Amma. The question I came up with was, how can I develop *vairagya* (dispassion)? She looked at me a little sternly and said, "You know that I didn't ask you to get a job to become like this. I wanted you to become strong on the path. But look at you. Look what you've become."

At that moment, I couldn't see that Amma had actually answered my question. She had basically said, "Son, look at how you are getting more and more engulfed by worldly life. But I know that if you continue to work hard, the nature of the world will be revealed to you, and eventually, you will gain vairagya. But maybe you should try a little harder." Had she said it in a sweet voice, I would have understood it, but it wouldn't have changed me. So, she said it in a way that would have a lasting impact. Amma was giving me the strength to take the next steps forward.

Slowly, unknown to me, she was moving me along the path that she had laid out for me. First, it was, come for all the US tours. Then, come to India for a couple of months every year. Then, spend six months a year with her. For 16 years, although I was moving ever closer to being with Amma full time, I still felt I was in a San Ramon exile, with little moments of peace to break it up. The more time I spent with Amma, the more difficult it became to live away from her. I felt helpless and depressed.

One morning, after a long night shift, I drove back to the San Ramon Ashram, too tired to even get out of the car. I fell asleep there. My phone rang. It was an international call. I picked it up hesitantly, wondering if there was some problem. It was Radhika-chechi.[5] She said that as there was too much work in the Western canteen, Amma wanted me to stay in the ashram and take over the cooking of the Western meals. I was speechless. Radhika-chechi, wondering if she had said something wrong, said, "You can take some time to think about it, if you want." I said, "No time needed. Bring me home! I want to come home!"

This time, when I came to Amritapuri, there was no mental agitation or fault finding. There was no fear because I was moving in Amma's time and in Amma's flow. The secret though is that Amma's time is actually our time; not the time that we want, but the time that Amma knows we need in order to succeed.

Amma gives us so many opportunities to attune ourselves to the place where she dwells. Her White Flowers of Peace and Ma-Om meditations are antidotes to the diseases of selfishness, fear and intolerance. These meditation techniques are a gift from a Mother to her children, from God to the world. And God, knowing our desperation, came in the form of a mother to show us the way. For who better than a mother can restore our child-like innocence, which allows us to accept everyone around us? Who better than a mother can tell us that we are greater than our biological and egotistical impulses, and that we can still live in harmony with nature? Who better than a mother can be that moral compass showing us the way ahead when we are lost?

---

[5] The person in charge of the International Office in the Amritapuri Ashram.

Who better than a mother can take us by the hand and lead us into the light?

Amma has shown us the path forward in a world ravaged by fear of the unknown, of COVID-19, and horrors yet unseen. It is love. We need only the courage to walk in it. Once we do, once we choose love, once we choose Amma, we will see that there, in Amma's flow, attuned to Amma's vibrations, all obstacles cease to exist. ༄

7

Wonder of Wonders
Bri. Shantipurnamrita Chaitanya

I heard about Amma long before I met her, but had to wait a long time for my first darshan.

In 1993, I learnt that Amma was visiting Kozhikode. As the Kozhikode Ashram was only a few miles away from where I lived, I decided to go and see her. My secret plan was not just to see Amma but to join her ashram also. I packed my belongings without anyone in the family noticing it. I thought that if Amma agreed, I would leave for the ashram at once. Unfortunately, during my darshan, I could not ask her anything. But Amma whispered in my ear, "My daughter, Amma understands your anguish. Don't worry. Amma is with you."

I had to wait another two years to ask Amma. All my family members opposed my idea of joining the ashram and thwarted all my attempts. Now, when I look back at the series of incidents leading up to my joining the ashram, I feel astonished. Isn't it amazing how Amma can change the course of our lives for the better? Every moment we spend with Amma is wonderful.

Lord Krishna says,

> *ashcaryavatpashyati kashcidenam ashcaryavadvadati canyah*
> *ashcaryavaccainamanyah shrrnoti shrutvapyenam veda na*
> *caiva kashcit*

Some see the Self as amazing. Some describe it as amazing. Some hear of it as amazing. Others, even on hearing, cannot understand it at all. (*Bhagavad Gita*, 2.29)

Similarly, the *Kathopanishad* declares:

shravanayapi bahubhiryo na labhyah shrnvanto'pi bahavo yam na vidyuh
ashcaryo vakta kushalo'sya labdha ashcaryo jnata kushalanushishtah

He about whom many are not even able to hear, whom many cannot comprehend even after hearing: wonderful is the teacher, wonderful is he who can receive when taught by an able teacher. (1.2.7)

Opportunities to hear about the Self are rare. If at all one hears about it, the chances of understanding what one hears are slim. It is said that only a handful in millions understands it rightly. The scriptures describe it as amazing because anything that cannot be perceived by our five sense organs is a wonder.

One must have an eye for beauty. Those who delight in seeing forests, the sunrise or sunset will intuit the glory of the Creator. These sights can transport such people to a state of rapture.

The scriptures say that the Self is '*anor aniyan mahato mahiyan*'—'smaller than the smallest, greater than the greatest.' The five sense organs can perceive only (external) objects, not the perceiving subject. In order to understand the perceiver, we must turn inward and the mind must become subtle. Just as we can see a clear reflection in a clean mirror, an uncluttered mind will be able to perceive the Self. It goes without saying that one needs the Guru's grace to have this inner vision.

Once, a teacher asked her students to name the seven wonders of the world. The students listed the Taj Mahal, Panama Canal, the Great Wall of China, etc. One student did not stop writing even after a long time. Surprised, the teacher went over to him to see what he was writing. He had listed altogether different things: hearing, talking, walking… When the teacher asked him why he considered them wonders, the boy replied that he had a brother who was born deaf and dumb. Hearing this, the teacher's eyes welled up with tears.

Truly, wonders are countless. Much of what we take for granted are wonders to others. For the lame, walking is a wonder. For the mute, speaking is a wonder. For the unhealthy, health is a wonder. Amma always reminds us that even the next breath is not in our hands; it rests in God's hands. So, even something as simple as breathing is a wonder. We are able to function by God's grace alone.

Some declare that Amma is powerful enough to make the lame climb a mountain. What this really means is that she instils self-confidence in that person. It might be possible to treat lameness surgically. But only *mahatmas* (spiritually illumined souls) like Amma can give someone who is physically challenged the confidence to scale a mountain. Only they can change the innate tendencies of our minds.

Before I joined the ashram, I had a close friend who committed suicide by jumping into a deep lake. One day when I was sleeping, I dreamt of her. It was a lucid dream. She came and sat next to me, and said that she was feeling desolate in her new world because hers had been an unnatural death. She asked me to join her by jumping into the same lake. I was horrified! I said, "You know that I'm going to Amma. I cannot join you." But she persisted.

To free myself from her clutches, I told her to leave, adding that I would join her when I die. But she shook me violently and kept repeating, "Come with me!" When I realized that she wouldn't leave me without taking me with her, I became frightened. I recalled Amma's words: "Daughter... don't worry. Amma is with you." Mustering all my strength and visualizing Amma, I screamed "Amma!" My late friend took her hands off me. When I screamed "Amma" a second time, she asked, "So you won't come with me?" When I called out to "Amma" yet again, she backed away from me and vanished into thin air. I woke up and saw my family members standing around me. I realized that I had really been screaming my lungs out.

One might think that this was just the overworking of my imagination, but for me, the experience was vivid even though I cannot explain it logically. I feel sure that if Amma had not saved me then, I would have left my house and followed my friend into the lake, for there had been such a strong bond between us. Even now, when I recall that episode, I still feel stunned. I had never told Amma about my friend's suicide, and was not physically near her at that time. But by merely uttering the great mantra "Amma" three times, I had been saved from the clutches of death. Who else other than Amma can work wonders like this?

Have you seen Amma during the arati or at the end of Devi Bhava? With a bewitching smile, Amma's eyes take everyone in. Isn't that gaze extraordinary? Everyone feels that Amma looked at them, even the person sitting at the back of the hall. Only she can look in that way.

There is a story in the *Bhagavata* of how Sage Narada wanted to test Lord Krishna. When he went to the private chambers of each of the 16,008 wives of the Lord, in each, he clearly saw the Lord in his physical form. He also saw Krishna feeding the cows, playing with children, chatting with the villagers... all at the same time. Seeing this, Narada became convinced of the Lord's all-pervasive and omnipotent nature.

Once, when Amma was giving darshan in the San Ramon Ashram, a devotee came with a parrot. Amma took the chirping bird in hand. Hearing its chirps, Amma told the devotee that he wanted a female companion. Soon, another devotee, who knew nothing about what Amma had said, brought a female parrot. Both birds joyfully rose to the roof and flew across the hall, chirping sweetly. The scene was truly wondrous. Amma is truly the mother of all beings, and that is why she could understand these birds.

Have we not heard stories of Lord Krishna appearing before the aged Kururamma (1570 – 1640), an ardent devotee of Guruvayurappa (a form of the Lord), and doing all her household chores? Are these just fables?

A swamini shared a wonderful experience that her mother had. Her mother had been asthmatic for a long time. Whenever her asthma worsened, the daughter would attend to all her needs. After the daughter joined the ashram, one day the mother's asthma became severe and she desperately needed help. But there was no one to get even a glass of water for her. At that point, her daughter's college friend walked into the house and asked how she was doing and whether she had eaten. The mother had not eaten anything. Sizing up the situation, the friend went to the kitchen and returned with some water for the mother to drink. She then made a few *dosas* (Indian pancakes). After feeding the mother, the friend cleaned the whole house. Just before leaving, she told the mother, "There is a lot of thatch lying about in the courtyard. I will come back another day to stack it properly." Saying so, she left. The mother was so grateful to her for the timely help, and thanked Amma for sending her.

After a few months, the mother went to Amritapuri. There, she saw the girl who had helped her when she was sick. She went up to her and said, "Daughter, you were such a big help for me the other day. But I haven't seen you since."

The girl looked perplexed. She asked, "When did I help you?"

The mother said, "Have you forgotten? Remember how you came to my house, made dosas for me and cleaned the house? You also said that you would come back another day to stack the thatch."

The girl said, "I never came to your house. Firstly, I don't know how to get there. Moreover, my parents would never allow me to go to friends' houses alone. How then could I have done all those things?"

The mother realized that Amma herself had come in the guise of her daughter's friend. Recalling all the work that had been done, the mother felt sad that Amma had gone to such lengths for her. Her eyes welled up with tears. Amma says that she is a servant of the servants of god. This experience proves it.

Many people wonder what their lives would have been like without Amma. Let me share one of my experiences. Some years ago, I developed an eye problem. When I consulted an eye specialist, he said that my eye had been afflicted by the chickenpox virus, and that I would lose my eyesight completely as there was no medicine for this condition. I was devastated. Mentally, I prayed to Amma. "Amma! How can I live my life without eyesight? How will I be able to see You? How will I move forward?"

Amma was abroad then. Her physical absence made me even more despondent. In those days, conveying a message to Amma was not easy. But someone managed to send word to Amma, who responded immediately. She asked me to go to the Aravind Eye Hospital in Madurai, Tamil Nadu. I consulted an ophthalmologist there. Right after I left for Madurai, Amma even called the ashram to find out if I had already left. I had to take medication for two months. Subsequently, the disease disappeared completely. On the day of my discharge, the doctor sent for me. He said, "I never thought you'd get back your vision. Only the grace of God brought you here at the right time and only because of divine grace was the treatment successful."

After Amma returned to the ashram, she called me and asked about my eyes and the treatment. I am convinced that it was by her grace alone that I regained my vision, thus enabling me to continue to see her and witness her divine play. How indebted we all are to Amma!

If we reflect on all that happens with and around Amma, we will become certain that she is not just a five-foot-tall woman. She is all-pervading and she is unfathomable. She is a wonder of wonders. ෨ð෧෨

8

Saving Grace
Br. Prabuddhamrita Chaitanya

Some scriptural terms are like the tip of an iceberg. There is so much more meaning to them than meets the eye. For example, take *'kamatkrodho'bhijayate'*—'from desire arises anger' (*Bhagavad Gita*, 2.62). To understand all its implications, we need to examine the whole verse:

> *dhyayato vishayanpumsah sangasteshupajayate*
> *sangatsanjayate kamah kamatkrodho'bhijayate*

When the mind dwells on an object, it develops an attachment to it. From attachment arises desire, and from desire arises anger...

The following verse completes this thought.

> *krodhadbhavati sammohah sammohatsmrtivibhramah*
> *smrti-bhramshad buddhinasho buddhinashatpranashyati*

...from anger arises delusion, delusion leads to a loss of memory; a loss of memory leads to an impairment of the intellect, which leads to one's ruin. (2.63)

These verses, incorporating many psychological principles, are rich in meaning and relevant to anyone and everyone. Here,

Lord Krishna explains in a step by step manner how a seemingly insignificant sensual thought can lead to total disaster. Even if a spiritual seeker thinks that he has gained control over his senses, as long as he has not attained spiritual liberation, the danger of a fall is ever present. Amma has even said that a seeker can experience a downfall a moment before God-realization.

A devotee once asked Amma, "Why is it that some seekers, even after joining the ashram, fall prey to *vasanas* (latent tendencies)?"

Amma replied, "What the Guru does is to bring out and expose the disciple's weaknesses, so that the disciple becomes aware of them and strives to overcome them. The Guru creates circumstances that stir the dormant impurities and makes the disciple conscious of them so that he can strive to rid himself of them."

Amma speaks about a type of snake in the Himalayas. Such snakes live in the frozen snow and do not attempt to bite anyone, but that is not their true nature. Once winter ends and the climate becomes warmer, the seemingly harmless snakes will show their true colors. Similarly, certain circumstances can bring out our true nature.

Let me recount an incident that makes me ashamed even now. Almost three decades ago, during my first darshan after joining the ashram, I asked Amma whether she would give me sannyasa. Amma smiled and asked me, "What do you think sannyasa is?"

Without the slightest doubt, I said, "A sannyasi is one who wears ochre robes, walks around chanting mantras, and sports *rudraksha* malas and bracelets." Such was my understanding!

Hearing this, Amma burst out laughing and said, "Son, that's not sannyasa! It does not mean dressing up at all. If you want to become a sannyasi, first burn away the dross from your mind and make it ochre. Only when that happens does one become a sannyasi."

Two weeks after this incident, I developed an aversion to the food served in the ashram, especially the curries. As far as I was concerned, there was no correlation between the curry's name and its taste! What I found most intolerable was the *sambar*. When I began to find it totally unpalatable, I began to consider leaving the ashram. I, who had expressed a desire to become a sannyasi just a few weeks before, was now ready to leave the spiritual life just because I could not stomach the sambar!

Then I thought, "Leaving the ashram without informing Amma is a sign of ingratitude!" I felt mentally perturbed and finally decided to speak to Amma. When I went for darshan, she repeatedly said, "Tell me, son. Tell me."

I opened up to Amma. I told her that I felt like leaving the ashram. Amma asked me why. With utmost shame, I told her that I was unable to stomach the curries served here, especially the sambar. Amma roared with laughter and asked me if I had come to the ashram to drink sambar. I could not say anything, and bent my head in shame. Then, pointing to her right, Amma said, "Son, sit here."

I sat by her side. Within 15 minutes, that thought, which had been upsetting me so much, disappeared from my mind completely, and has never bothered me again. I realized that the mere presence of a *mahatma* (spiritually illumined soul) has the power to purify.

The scriptures clearly warn of the dangers of sensual pleasures and of the need to subdue the mind, but only a Guru can discern the spiritual state of a seeker and guide him or her accordingly. So, even if one has considerable scriptural knowledge, one still needs the guidance of a Guru. Only she can rectify the deficiencies in a seeker and lead him or her to Self-realization. Without the Guru's grace, the disciple will undoubtedly perish.

Let me recount one of my experiences. Years ago, I had an ardent lover—a slim, white foreigner. Her name was Marlboro... yes, it was a cigarette! I was a chain smoker, and eventually contracted mouth cancer. I underwent treatment for a long time and finally reached a critical phase when I knew that I would have to choose between cigarettes and life. When I realized that I could not give up the habit, I decided to go and see Amma, at the instigation of a friend.

I went to the Kodungallur Brahmasthanam Temple with four cartons of cigarettes, a matchbox, an air pillow, five pillow covers, and a couple of bedsheets. When I reached the temple, my friend made me register for the *Lalita Sahasranama archana* (chanting of the 1,000 names of the Divine Mother). The devotees were accommodated in Amma's school (Amrita Vidyalayam) in Kodungallur. I was given a mat for sleeping. For a pillow, at first, I used the cigarette cartons. I concealed them by covering them with my towel. I kept at least a few cigarette packets with me so that I could smoke during the intervals between each chanting of the *Lalita Sahasranama* which went on from dawn to dusk. I was totally convinced that even God could not stop my urge to smoke. So, while everyone else was chanting *"Om parashaktyai namah"* ("Salutations to the Almighty Goddess") after each mantra of the *Lalita Sahasranama*, I chanted a very different mantra: "O God, at least in my next birth, please ensure that I don't have this bad habit of smoking!"

I finished all the cigarettes that I had brought to the program by the morning of the last day of the programs. On that day, after the first archana, I went to a nearby teashop to buy cigarettes. As I couldn't find the brand of cigarettes I wanted, I had no choice but to buy a different brand. I bought all 10 packets available in that shop. The shopkeeper also gave me a matchbox. I tried to light a cigarette but somebody behind me strongly blew away the flame. When I turned around, there was no one there. I turned to another direction and tried to light it again, and the same thing happened. I went on trying until I had exhausted the last matchstick in the box. Some invisible force was blowing the fire away! But this made me even more determined. I went to the lit stove used for making tea, and thought to myself, "If anyone is capable of blowing this away, let him or her try!"

Suddenly, at that moment, I heard an inner voice, Amma's voice, commanding me sternly to throw the cigarettes away. I threw away all the 10 packets of cigarettes, including the cigarette between my lips. I paid for the cigarettes and walked towards the Brahmasthanam Temple.

Later that night, I joined the queue for Amma's darshan. When I reached her, I didn't say anything. Amma also did not say anything to me, but I could feel the power of her penetrating gaze as it fell on my body. After darshan, I returned to the school and laid down. Because of my illness, I used to change the pillow covers frequently at night. That night, too, in a half-asleep state, I touched my pillow. To my surprise, I did not feel the wetness of the blood-clotted pus and saliva that used to ooze out of my mouth. Wonderstruck, I went to the bathroom, stood before the mirror, opened my mouth, and looked inside. My inner cheeks had become as fleshy as they used to be before the cancer struck. I could not believe it! At first, I thought that Amma might have performed some black magic to create this illusion, but I soon realized that Amma had healed me purely by her *sankalpa* (divine resolve).

However, for the longest time, even after I joined the ashram, I could not shake away the sense of disbelief at what had happened. At around this time, Amma was about to leave for her North Indian Tour. It was the second such tour after I joined the ashram, and I was expecting my name to be in the list of brahmacharis accompanying Amma on the tour. It was not. Though disappointed, I consoled myself, thinking that I would get a chance the following year. But the same thing continued to happen in the years that followed...

With each passing year, the disbelief began to grow stronger. But I did not disclose this to Amma. After four years, when I saw that my name was still not on the list whereas the name of a brahmachari who had just joined the ashram was, I became disillusioned. I felt that it was probably because Amma did not have faith in me and that she did not want such people to accompany her.

On the one hand, I loved Amma, but on the other hand, I was frustrated and sad. Gradually, this frustration turned into contempt for ashram life. But owing to my love for Amma, I couldn't bear to leave the ashram either. Finally, I decided to test Amma. I thought, if Amma is truly Parashakti (the Almighty Goddess), then she should know my mind. I decided that I would continuously chant a mantra that I had composed from 6 a.m. to 5 p.m. on the day Amma was leaving for the tour; I would eat nothing and only drink water in that time. I wanted Amma to tell me that mantra I was chanting before she left for the tour. If she did, I would never disbelieve Amma ever again; nor would I ever leave her. But if Amma failed this test, I would leave the ashram as soon as she left for the tour.

I began chanting at 6 o'clock in the morning of the day Amma was leaving. I chanted without moving my lips or without any sound. I drank some water in the afternoon and continued chanting until the evening. The mantra that I had composed and which Amma was supposed to tell me was, "Even if your name is not on the list of brahmacharis accompanying Amma for the

North Indian tour, you should come for Amma's Kodungallur program."

After my chanting ended, I went for the evening bhajans, ate dinner, and returned to my hut. My roommate asked me to wake him up at 11 p.m. and went to sleep. I sat outside on the verandah. The night was bright with moonlight and there was pin-drop silence. Suddenly, a brahmachari came to me and sympathetically asked, "Brother, you're not going on the tour, are you?"

Hiding my grief, I told him, "I can go next year." He then told me that he would come near the car with Swamiji's bags shortly before Amma left and he would then let me know exactly when Amma was leaving. He added, "You'll get a darshan of Amma without the usual crowd. So, be happy."

I continued sitting there, feeling anger towards the whole universe. At around 11 o'clock, the tour buses arrived. The ashram residents going for the tour boarded the buses, which started leaving at 11:30 p.m. After that, Amma's car was parked near where the main stage is now. The brahmachari who had promised to tell me Amma's departure time informed me that Amma was leaving in five minutes. He also showed me where I could wait and have her darshan.

As soon as he left, I went and hid behind a screen of plants and trees, near where the Indian canteen is now. Amma would never find me there. I did not want her to see me either. I then saw Amma walking towards the car; a few people were with her. When I saw her, I reverentially prostrated and mentally bid her farewell. My heart was beating so loudly that I could hear it. Amma opened the door to the car and put one leg inside. I was peering through the leaves. I saw Amma remaining in that position for some time. Suddenly, Amma withdrew her leg and started looking around. Turning around, she started running towards my hideout. I thought she was looking for someone else

who might have been longing for her darshan. She came around
the plants where I was hiding and held me close to her. She asked,
"Son, are you so sad because you're not able to go for the tour?"

I couldn't say anything but began to cry. Then Amma whispered into my ears, "After the Indian tour, Amma has a program
in Kodungallur. You can come for that."

All my doubts ceased. Amma knows everything. She creates
all the circumstances.

The seva that Amma gives us will help us overcome our
vasanas. No matter how much effort we put in, we can overcome
our vasanas only by the Guru's grace. Doing one's seva sincerely
will make us deserving of her grace.

The Guru's greatest miracle is elevating the disciple from the
state of incompleteness to completeness. The Guru-disciple lore
is replete with instances of Gurus uplifting souls from the pit
of self-destruction to the heights of Self-realization. Because a
Guru is all-knowing, a *jitakami* (one who has subdued desires),
an epitome of all noble qualities, and a knower of the Truth, the
disciple who is ready to obey her words unquestioningly becomes
eligible for Self-realization. If we do not like the seva that the
Guru has assigned us, our *sadhana* (spiritual practice) is to learn
to like it.

As the process of inner purification is long and as the seeker
is prone to downfalls, the Guru's presence is very important. The
senses are more powerful than we realize and they can easily trap
a seeker. He or she should regard sense pleasures as poison and
relinquish them.

Sensual thoughts are the cause of a spiritual downfall.
When the desires arising from the constant dwelling upon such
thoughts are thwarted, we become enraged. This wrath will lead
to indiscriminate behavior. The deluded state of mind paves the

way to forgetfulness, which will destroy the intellect, and thus seal our fate.

Once, a scientist wanted to make a discovery that would benefit the whole of mankind. He thought that if he could convert seawater into fuel, there would be a permanent solution to the energy crisis facing the whole world. Many rich friends came forward to help him financially. A laboratory to conduct experiments was set up in the USA. Many famous scientists came forward to assist him. Despite trying continuously for 15 years, he did not succeed. Those who came to help him gradually left, one by one.

But a friend in India with whom he used to exchange emails stood by him. When the scientist stopped communicating with him, the friend decided to visit the scientist. When he reached the laboratory, the scientist told him that he was going to abandon further research as all his efforts had led him to a dead end. The friend said, "Do not give up. Go and see a Lama in Tibet and ask for a solution. Your problems will be solved and your research will be fruitful." The friend added that there were three conditions attached to the consultation: 1. he should frame the problem in a single sentence; 2. he should walk to the abode of the Lama, continuously chanting that question like a mantra; 3. he would be allowed to ask just one question.

The scientist agreed to all these conditions and went to see the Lama with great expectations. When he reached the Lama's residence, the watchman told him, "Follow this path. It will lead you to a small hill. Climb that hill, which has 108 steps. At each step, recite the question that you want to ask the Lama. Once you reach the top of the hill, you will find the Lama sitting there. On seeing you, the Lama will ask you to ask the question to which you want an answer. Remember, you will not get an opportunity to ask another question."

The scientist did as instructed. After he had climbed all the 108 steps, he saw a young and extremely beautiful woman seated on a golden throne. He was surprised because he had been expecting an old, wizened man with a long, flowing beard. The Lama asked the scientist, "What is your question?"

The question that the scientist had planned to ask the Lama was "How to convert seawater into fuel?" Instead, he asked, "Madam, are you married?"

This story illustrates the strength of vasanas. Even on our deathbed, these vasanas can create havoc. Only the Guru's grace can save us in such situations. May Amma mercifully shower her grace on all of us and help us overcome all such situations. ☙

9

Instrument in Her Hands

Br. Sharanamrita Chaitanya

What does it mean to be an instrument in the hands of the Divine? The following verse from the *Bhagavad Gita* gives us a clear idea:

> *tasmat tvam uttishtha yasho labhasva*
> *jitva shatrun bhunkshva rajyam samrddham*
> *mayaivaite nihatah purvam eva*
> *nimitta-matram bhava savya-sacin*

> Therefore, arise and attain fame. Conquer your enemies and enjoy the prosperous kingdom. I have already killed these warriors. O master archer, just be an instrument of my work. (11.33)

Lord Krishna had already done the work that Arjuna had been deputed to do. The Lord was merely bestowing on Arjuna the blessed opportunity of being an instrument in his hands.

Amma often tells us to be like a brush in the hands of an artist or a pen in the hands of a poet. She also shows us how to be one, just as Krishna guided Arjuna in the battlefield of Kurukshetra. If she asks us to do something, she will also show us how to do so. However, if we egoistically feel that we are the real doers, we can expect to face sorrow.

I have been blessed to act as an instrument in Amma's hands on many occasions. Let me recount one instance. About 10 years ago, we helped Amrita Television organize an award ceremony. Amrita TV was an enterprise started by devotees of Amma who wanted to leverage the outreach a TV channel would have, to promote spiritual values among the masses. The award ceremony was to take place on the grounds outside the Jawaharlal Nehru International Stadium in Kochi, Kerala. The date was finalized, advertisements were placed, and about 7,000 event passes were distributed. The function was to take place in June. Amma was in the US then. From the day the preparations for the event started, it started raining heavily, making the grounds of the venue muddy and water-logged. The function was to take place in 48 hours, but the stage had not been erected and the chairs had not been arranged. What to do? The then CEO, an ardent devotee of Amma, called Swami Amritaswarupananda and told him that the program would have to be called off because of the unrelenting rains. Swamiji informed Amma, who called me and told me to go to the venue and do whatever was necessary. I was apprehensive. How would I manage this? However, I remembered how Amma had helped me in similar situations earlier.

When I reached the venue with two other brahmacharis, I saw workers sitting in the rain, not knowing what to do. We had only 24 hours left! Amma called and gave us instructions over the phone. We gathered the workers and somehow managed to build the stage, but there was still knee-level water on the grounds. Amma asked us to create embankments on all sides of the grounds to prevent water from entering. She then asked us to dig small pits, pump out the water from these pits, and to use jute sacks to dry the grounds. We spent all night doing this.

On the day of the event, Amma called at around 3 p.m. I told her that it was still raining, and that only if we started arranging the chairs by 3:30 p.m. could we finish in time for the function at 6 pm. There was a minute of silence, and then Amma said, "You can start placing the chairs soon. Amma will call after some time." At 3:30 p.m. sharp, the rains stopped as if someone had turned off a switch! Together with a hundred other workers, we used jute sacks to dry the grounds and arrange the chairs. People arrived, and the program proceeded smoothly, ending at around 9:30 p.m. As soon as the invitees left, it started raining again! We all were convinced that what had happened was Amma's *lila* (divine play), and we had been blessed with an opportunity to play a small part in it.

When our actions are aligned to her will, what follows are joy and peace. Becoming an instrument in God's hands does not mean sitting idly but acting with dedication and discernment. Amma always reminds us that only by divine grace can we do even the smallest deed. A puppet might think people are applauding and appreciating its actions, but the truth is that it is nothing without the puppeteer, who pulls the strings. Similarly, we must have the attitude that all our 'strength' is only the play of divine power.

Whatever the Guru asks us to do is for our benefit, no matter how small it may be. We must do it with the strong conviction that it is for our spiritual growth.

Once, Amma called me and asked me to do some work. Because of my ego, I did not do it properly. When Amma found out about this, she did not say anything. She stopped talking to me altogether! How much more preferable her scolding would have been. Words cannot express the pain I felt on being ignored by Amma. I wrote many letters of apology to her but received no response. I continued my seva (selfless service) as telephone operator. Previously, if Amma wanted to find out something, she would call me. Now, she began sending someone to get the information. If Amma wanted to call someone, she would send someone to dial the number and connect the call to Amma. This continued for a while. I became so perturbed that I could neither sleep nor eat.

This was in September. Amma's birthday was just five days away. One evening, I learnt that after bhajans, Amma was going to visit the site of the birthday celebrations to check on the preparations. Previously, I had always accompanied Amma on these trips and would receive her instructions on what needed to be improved or changed. Realizing that I would not be a part of this cherished opportunity, my anguish reached its peak. I lost all control, ran to Amma's room, and started crying outside her door. That evening, when Amma returned to her room, she would have stepped on my tears on each of the steps leading to her room. I could not stop crying even after I returned to my room.

At around 9:30 p.m., Amma came down from her room and asked one of her attendants where I was. When she called me to tell me that Amma had asked for me, I ran to Amma, who took me to the birthday venue and started discussing the arrangements to be made, as if nothing had happened. Sometimes, the Master's silence teaches us huge lessons.

A doctor does not stop treating a patient just because the treatment might cause the patient some pain. The doctor's intention is only to heal him of the disease. Similarly, some of Amma's ways might cause us a little pain but it is only for our own good. The Guru's main goal is to remove the disciple's ego. To do so, she uses different methods, depending on the nature of the disciple. Just as a sculptor chips away at unwanted parts of the stone to create a beautiful idol, the Guru, out of pure compassion, removes all the unwanted tendencies obstructing the disciple's spiritual progress. We must try our best to give in. Without surrender, it is difficult to attain divine grace.

Before I started staying in Amritapuri, I was taking care of a small textile shop in Vaikom, Kerala. I had to take up the responsibility of managing this shop while I was still in 11th grade. The business was saddled with many debts and legal issues, but I thought I could manage this somehow. I prayed to Amma only for her blessings but did not tell her about the problems. After three years, the problems became insurmountable. I went for darshan and tearfully unburdened all my worries before Amma. I told her that I was helpless and that only Amma could resolve the problems. Consoling me, she said, "Amma will take care of all your problems. Don't worry, Amma is always with you."

True enough, all the problems were settled within a year. When we surrender everything at her feet, Amma will take care of all our needs. With no interest in continuing the business, I came to Amma and settled down in Amritapuri.

Someone asked a flute, "How does such beautiful music flow out from you?"

The flute replied, "I was just a bamboo pole. My master picked me up one day, cleaned me, put seven holes in me, removed the unwanted parts, and started playing me."

This is what Amma is trying to do with all of us. All we have to do is surrender. During Lord Rama's time, the *vanaras* (monkey companions) could be with the Lord only during the war. During Lord Krishna's lifetime, the *gopis* (milkmaids) and other ardent devotees like Akrura and Uddhava could not spend too much time with him. But we are blessed to be able to spend so much time with Amma. May our association with Amma continue and grow stronger. ☙

10

The Boat of our Lives

Swamini Suvidyamrita Prana

Once, an experienced captain of a ship set out on a voyage after extensive preparation. He was proud of his abilities, and his arrogance was evident in his behavior and attitude. Though this irritated his crew members, they had no choice but to obey his commands. The ship sailed as planned and the people aboard enjoyed their time on the sea.

One day, the weather suddenly changed. Dark rainclouds filled the sky and the waters became turbulent. As the ship began listing dangerously, the passengers began screaming. The captain shouted, "I'm here! Why are you afraid?" But when the ship began to lurch and sway alarmingly, the captain realized that matters were beyond his control. He looked up at the sky helplessly and joined his hands in prayer. He felt his vision clouding over and he fell unconscious.

After some time, the captain regained consciousness. There was complete silence. He looked around and saw that the ship was almost completely wrecked. No one other than him was on board. He screamed in desperation, but his cries were heard only by the sky and ocean waves. As he contemplated his earlier arrogance and his present helplessness, he was moved to prayer.

Suddenly, he heard a sound. When he opened his eyes, he saw a huge, white bird flying towards him. He realized that the ship must be near land. Summoning all his reserves of energy, he dived into the ocean and swam. He followed the direction of the bird and finally reached ashore.

We are all like the captain in the story. We start the journey of life with all kinds of plans and dreams. But unexpected storms devastate our hopes, and we are left floundering on the rising and falling waves of our *prarabdha* (past karma). Not knowing how to move ahead, we surrender helplessly. That is when, like the white bird in the story, supreme consciousness appears before us in the form of the Guru to guide us to safety. If we have faith in her and follow the path she shows us, divine grace will help us cross the ocean of transmigration (cycle of birth and death) and thus save us.

A gripping example of how the Lord saved a helpless soul can be seen in the *Bhagavad Gita*. Arjuna, who had been so proud of his abilities, suddenly became confused and began to despair. He cried out, "O Lord! I am Your disciple and surrender to You. Please guide and instruct me" (2.7).

Lord Krishna's response (in chapter 2) is the essence of the entire *Bhagavad Gita*. Among the gems of advice He gives Arjuna is the following:

yoga-sthah kuru karmani sangam tyaktva dhananjaya
siddhy-asiddhyoh samo bhutva samatvam yoga ucyate

Be steadfast in yoga, O Arjuna. Perform your duty
and abandon all attachment to success or failure. Such
evenness of mind is called yoga. (2.48)

Through this verse, Sri Krishna gives us a precise explanation of *karma yoga*, the path of dedicated action to God. Yoga is evenness of mind. It means freeing ourselves from the expectation of a particular outcome, remaining steady in the face of profit or loss, success or failure, and doing all actions with detachment. Amma conveys the same idea when she says, "Children, live in the present moment and do your duty. The present moment alone is in our hands. Whatever may come our way, move forward with courage. Leave the rest to God's will."

In 2006, after Amma left for the US Tour, I received a message: Amma wanted me to manage the Hyderabad Amrita Vidyalayam (school). It felt as if I had been smacked behind the head. Amma normally sends people who know the local language to specific places. Everyone, not just me, was surprised when Amma wanted me to go to Hyderabad, as I do not know Telugu at all. All the same, I was happy that Amma thought of me. Later, she herself instructed me on what exactly I was to do there and how I should conduct myself. I had faith that Amma would take care of everything.

At school, many problems would arise daily. Every morning, I would feel stressed anticipating the complaints and problems I would hear that day. But each problem would somehow be resolved, and I would be amazed. On reflection, there was only one explanation: Amma's grace was at work. She often tells us, "Children, don't stress yourself out. Try your best and leave the rest to God's will."

Amma can easily pay more qualified people to do much of the work the ashram does. What she is trying to do is not to create career professionals out of us. Amma is helping us gain an attitude of surrender. To do so, we must wholeheartedly try to do what Amma has deemed best for our spiritual progress.

Once, I took the school children to a fair and enjoyed watching them have fun on the Ferris wheel. However, one child in the group started screaming and crying to stop the wheel. This wheel was controlled by a switch. Once we get in, we can get off only after the switch is turned off. Whether we enjoy the ride or scream in fear, the switch will turn off only as previously determined. Similarly, the Creator has predetermined the beginning, middle and end of the Ferris wheel of our life. There is only one thing we can do: set a goal and strive to attain it. We must remember that the higher our goal, the more obstacles we will face and the larger the obstacles will be.

The Ganges flows from the high peaks of the Himalayas to the Bay of Bengal. Is her journey easy? No. She glides over small pebbles, negotiates huge boulders, drifts through and around trees that have fallen in her path, and navigates her way through mountain ranges. Does she ever think, "I can't do this! I've had enough!" No, no such thoughts ever arise. She flows without wavering, always surging ahead until she reaches her goal. We should also develop this firm determination and faith in our lives.

Such mental strength does not come easily to ordinary people, but it is the very nature of divine beings like Amma. Since childhood, she has had to face intense criticism from all quarters. Yet she remains unperturbed. It is mentioned in Amma's *Ashtottaram* (108 attributes) that Amma was silent when she emerged from her mother's womb (mantra 24). That silence was an expression of her inner equipoise. It is from this state of inner silence and balance that she does everything. All of Amma's charities are expressions of wisdom born of this even-mindedness. Whether it is disaster management or clean-up projects, orphanages or hospitals, relief or research projects, Amma quietly steers everything with unerring wisdom. She takes credit for nothing, receives both applause and criticism with detachment, and continues her mission of loving and serving others.

I heard about the following incident from Dr. Priya Nair. It took place after Amma was awarded an Honorary Doctorate by the State University of New York in 2010. After the award ceremony, Amma was taken to a room behind the stage. Priya was holding the ceremonial gown. Suddenly, Swami Amritas-warupananda took it from her, held it up to Amma, and excitedly said, "Dr. Amma! Dr. Amma! Amma has become a doctor!" Priya started clapping. But Amma put the robes aside and said, "What are you saying? I'm not interested in such titles! Amma does not do anything for awards. Today, people will applaud and tomorrow they might shout in criticism. What's the point in getting affected by either? Amma has agreed to accept this award because it makes you and my other children happy. But if you become attached to such so-called successes, you will become miserable when people criticize you. Remain calm."

What if we receive such an award? We would post photographs of ourselves on Facebook and try to get as many 'likes' as possible!

In fact, Amma demonstrates the entire *Bhagavad Gita* through her life. She continues to follow her dharma, disregarding both praise and insult, acceptance or rejection.

Amma has never cancelled darshans or tours, saying that she is tired. Even now, while the entire world is in lockdown, Amma remains as active as ever, even more so than before, as she reviews the affairs of each and every one of the branch ashrams all over the world.

I would like to share another incident, mentioned in Swami Ramakrishnananda's book *Amritashtakam*. When Amma visited Japan in 2011, Japan was still recovering from the Tohoku earthquake. The people travelling with Amma had not wanted her to go to Japan at all, and were relieved that the program venue was far from the earthquake's epicenter. Many people from relief camps came for Amma's darshan. Seeing their expressions, which were laden with anxiety, fear and desperation, Amma summoned the brahmachari overseeing the Japanese program and said, "Tomorrow, I'm going to the epicenter to see my children there. Make the necessary arrangements!"

After a long journey, Amma reached the local relief camps, embraced the refugees, and spent time with them. All those who were with her witnessed the courage and compassion of a true yogi. She then went to the nearby seashore and prayed for the souls of all those who had died and for harmony between humanity and nature. Such is her equal vision and love for all beings. Amma somehow managed to reach the next city just before the program was about to begin.

How is Amma able to do all this? She exists in a state beyond the body, mind and intellect, but comes down to our level in order to guide us. The scriptures state that we must learn and follow the examples of spiritual masters.

We can learn the following from Amma. These are the factors that transform karma into karma yoga:

- Enjoy all the actions we perform.
- Give more importance to the effort than to the result of actions.
- Remain detached from the results of action. Do not become elated by success or dejected by failure. Accept everything as *prasad*, a gift from God. This is surrender.

When we see a half-filled glass, we could say that it is half full or half empty. Which is correct? The truth is that the glass is half water and half emptiness. Likewise, we must see everything for what it is.

Once, when Amma was returning to her room after darshan, a devotee offered her three yellow roses from her garden. Amma looked at the flowers for a few moments, enjoyed their fragrance, and then said with a smile, "The shape and petals of these roses are so different, and yet, each one is so beautiful." After a few moments of silence, Amma continued, "You know, when I look at the world, I see everything like these flowers: so different, yet so exquisitely beautiful! Each and every one of you, every person that comes for darshan, each person who passes by, is so different yet so divinely beautiful. If only you could see the world the way I do..."

We cannot even begin to imagine what this state is like. Amma is that rare soul who beholds only beauty. From that rarefied position, whom could we hate? How could we be sad when there is only beauty? There would be nothing negative, only a constant flow of positive energy. There will only be love and compassion for all. Amma sings:

> *taye! nin makkalanennuracchal*
> *loka vairuddhyam snehamakum...*
> *dharmam engum anandam ekum* (from '*Shakti Rupe*')

O Mother, if one looks upon all as your children, the contradictions of the world will be transformed into love, and righteousness will spread joy everywhere!

Earlier in this article, life was compared to a ship on a mighty ocean. Let us have the faith that the boats of our lives are sailing on Amma's ocean of bliss. Then, no matter how strong the hurricanes or storms may be, there will be nothing to fear. We need never be anxious about the future either.

Let us live without fear, filled only with the prayer, "Never let me stray from you!" May Amma fulfil this prayer. ᕙᕗ

11

The Lord's Guarantee

Br. Devidasa Chaitanya

In the *Bhagavad Gita*, Lord Krishna offers these words of assurance:

> *kshipram bhavati dharmatma shashvacchantim nigacchati*
> *kaunteya pratijanihi na me bhaktah pranashyati*

> My devotee soon becomes righteous and attains eternal peace. O Arjuna, rest assured, my devotee never perishes. (9.31)

The phrase *'na me bhakta pranashyati'* literally means, "My devotee never perishes." This can mean that God saves devotees from dangers and looks after their needs. Does it also mean that a true devotee is immortal or that he or she will never feel any misery? But the lives of many great devotees show how they faced difficulties and suffered as a result. How can we reconcile this seeming contradiction?

The *Bhagavad Gita* refers to four kinds of devotees: the *arta, artharthi, jijnasu* and *jnani*, i.e. the distressed, the seeker of wealth, the seeker of (divine) knowledge, and the knower of Truth. In the verse mentioned earlier, the Lord is referring to the third and fourth kinds.

Amma speaks about *'tattvattile bhakti'* — devotion based on an understanding of spiritual principles. Devotees with that understanding know that problems are part of life, and they take them in their stride. They do not see even death as a tragedy but as a reunion with his Beloved.

Prahlada, an ardent devotee of Lord Vishnu, is tormented by his father Hiranyakashipu, who wants his son to relinquish his devotion to the Lord. But Prahlada refuses, and the father tries to kill him in many ways: by hurling him off a cliff, throwing him into a river, tossing him before a stampeding elephant... Every time, the Lord saves Prahlada. Finally, Hiranyakashipu unsheathes his sword to kill the child and asks him, "Where is your Vishnu to protect you now?"

Prahlada's devotion was grounded in *jnana* (knowledge). He replies: "My Lord is everywhere, even in these pillars around us."

Outraged, Hiranyakashipu strikes one of the pillars with the sword. The Lord emerges from that pillar as Narasimha and kills Hiranyakashipu.

God does not always save devotees from death. When Jatayu, a giant eagle and ardent devotee of Lord Rama, saw Ravana, the demon king, abducting Sita, he tried to stop the demon. But the king hacked away the wings of the bird, who fell from the sky. Before Jatayu breathed his last, Lord Rama arrived, took Jatayu onto His lap, and lavished him with love and affection in his last moments. Thus, Jatayu attained liberation.

In supreme devotion, the Lord and devotee become one spiritually. This is the state referred to in the prayer, *'Mrityorma amritam gamaya'*—'Lead me from death to immortality.' The *Narada Bhakti Sutras* describes the state of true devotion thus: *'Yal labdhva puman... amrito bhavati'*—'Attaining which, one becomes immortal' (4). In this state, the question of God protecting His devotee does not arise, for the protector (God) and protected (devotee) are one.

Many of Amma's children have experiences of how she saved them from difficulties in their lives. Swami Dayamritananda shared one such experience with me. He came to Amma in the early 80's, not as a devotee but out of curiosity. During his very first Devi Bhava darshan, he saw Amma receiving Dattan, the leper. As she drew him into her arms, Amma's eyes were filled with love. She then began licking the oozing wounds, sucking the pus out from them. This scene made a profound impact on the future swami, who soon decided to join the ashram.

But Amma wanted him to obtain permission from his parents first. Unfortunately, they wanted him to lead a 'normal' life. In order to divert him from spirituality, his parents decided to send him abroad, where his relatives were entrusted to look after him. When Swami told Amma about this, she said, "Go now. You will face many situations that will test you. If you remain unswerving, Amma will make a *sankalpa* (divine resolve), and you will be able to come back soon."

Swami went abroad and stayed there for a couple of years. He had to face many challenges, but with inner strength derived from his love for Amma, remained steadfast throughout. Seeing his unresponsiveness to the temptations of worldly life, his relatives were ready to give up. Swami pleaded with them to buy him an air ticket so that he could return to India. They refused.

Dayamritananda Swami was left in the lurch. He did not have sufficient money to buy a ticket. Wondering what to do, he rummaged through his suitcase and found an old Air India return ticket, which was well past the expiry date. Hoping against hope, he went to the Air India office, approached a woman at the counter, and asked if there was any way that he could redeem the ticket. She looked at it and right away said, "No way!"

Heartbroken, Dayamritananda Swami silently called out to Amma for help even as he remained standing in the Air India

Office. After a few moments, the same woman called out to him from behind the counter: "Maybe we can give it a try. Do you have records of any recent medical treatment you underwent? If you do, there might be a way out."

Call it a sheer coincidence (or Amma's grace). Swami had undergone medical treatment for his eyes not long before and had the relevant papers in his bag! Within a few minutes, the return ticket to India (and the spiritual life) was in his hands.

Amma personally helped me appreciate the meaning of '*na me bhakta pranashyati*' through an experience. Shortly after joining the ashram in 1991, Amma sent me to AICT (Amrita Institute of Computer Technology), the ashram's computer training institute in Puthiyakavu. I was to study there and help Dr. Krishnakumar, who was in charge of the institute then. As part of my work, I had to go outside for purchases. While passing shops selling eatables, the desire to eat those items would arise. Ashram life then was much more austere: drinking tea was frowned upon, reading newspapers was regarded as a waste of time, and eating food from outside was a big no-no. But the desire to eat delectable snacks grew day by day.

One day, I saw some peanuts in a shop. Unable to resist the temptation, I went into the shop and bought a packet of peanuts. After dinner, I ate the peanuts, all the while feeling guilty. This sense of unease and guilt kept increasing. After a few days, I could not bear it any longer. I went to Amma, trembling within, and told her what I had done. She looked at me sternly and said, "If you don't have any *vairagya* (dispassion) even at the beginning of your ashram life, how will you stick to this path?"

I walked away with a heavy heart. The days that followed were difficult. I tried hard to intensify my *sadhana* (spiritual practices). I would fast one day and overeat the next. I was struggling with my *vasanas* (latent tendencies), failing often, and feeling miserable as a result. I began to feel that I was not fit for the spiritual path. At the same time, worldly life looked dreadful and I could not imagine returning to it. Feeling forlorn, I thought that perhaps it was time to end my life.

One evening, during bhajans, Amma sang many poignant songs such as *'Kannunir toratta ravukal etra poyi'* ('How many nights have I passed with eyes overflowing with tears?') and *'Ente kannunir etra kandalum manassaliyuka ille'* ('Though seeing my tears, how is it You feel no compassion?'). These songs seemed to reflect my inner state. I cried throughout the bhajans.

After bhajans, I went to sit on the western veranda of the Kali temple, facing the balcony of Amma's room. I wanted to meditate but could not stop crying. I felt I had reached the end of my tether. As I cried, I was fervently praying, "O Amma, am I really unworthy of this spiritual path? Won't you give me one more chance and save me from this misery? I just don't think I can hold on any more...."

A couple of hours must have gone by. The entire area was dark, except for a small light in Amma's room. Suddenly, the beam from a flashlight fell on my face. Opening my eyes, I saw that it was coming from Amma's balcony. It was Amma holding the flashlight! She asked, "Who's that?"

With a frail voice, I said, "Amma, it's me..."

She kept the light on my face for some time before switching it off. After a few moments, Amma beamed the light on my face again. She also threw something at me. It was an apple. Amma's *prasad*! She then spoke, this time softly and lovingly: "Hey Sudeep! Eat that now and go to sleep. And get up for archana tomorrow."

It was the first time Amma had called me by my name! I felt as if I had rediscovered myself. Amma had known me all along. She had heard all my prayers and seen all the tears rolling down my cheeks. She had understood and felt all my inner pangs of anguish. And she had accepted me in her heart… The relief and tranquility I felt were inexpressible.

I continued crying while eating the apple. I then returned to my hut and cried until I fell asleep. They were tears of gratitude.

When I woke up the next day, I was a new person. My self-confidence had been restored, and my heart was filled with Amma's love.

In all my years with Amma, this incident still stands out as the most engrossing for me. I had been fumbling in the darkness. The apple and Amma lovingly calling me by my name epitomized, for me, Lord Krishna's assurance to Arjuna: *'na me bhakta pranashyati.'* Amma conveys the same sentiment, in a warmer way, when she whispers in our ears, "My darling son/daughter, do not worry. Mother is always with you."

In hindsight, I realize that the experience was not about peanuts at all but about my inner struggle to rise up to my spiritual aspirations. At that time, I considered my craving for tasty food a serious problem. The real issue was my inability to overcome the weaknesses of my mind. This was a big blow to my ego, and my repeated failures led to a loss of self-confidence. Amma's response to my confession had only reflected my own sense of failure; it was not a reflection of her attitude towards food. The mask of sternness she wore helped me arrive at a more realistic understanding of how to balance desire with the fundamental values of the spiritual life.

It is important for a spiritual seeker to hold fast to spiritual values and to the routine of spiritual practices. As Amma often reminds us, even a minuscule hole in a boat can cause it to capsize. Unless we ensure that the boat of our spiritual life is leak-free, how can we cross the ocean of *samsara*, the cycle of births and deaths?

Amma is *'ahaituka kripa sindhu'*—the ocean of causeless mercy. She is a *kalpataru*, the divine, wish-fulfilling tree, which fulfils longings that take us closer to God. She does not expect anything from us. Nevertheless, let us offer to her our pure and sincere prayers, prayers that reach her heart of divine love. Through *shraddha* (faith and attentiveness) and bhakti, may we all become one with Amma and attain her divine abode of immortality. ෧๑๑

12

Taming the Mind
Bri. Gurukripamrita Chaitanya

Amma says that there can be heavy traffic on the road sometimes; at other times, it will be clear. But the traffic of thoughts in the mind—a continuous stream of thoughts, worries, hopes, dreams, regrets, judgments, and so forth—never abates. Though we might be in India, our mind can be in New York. Such is the nature of an untamed mind. It is never still. It thinks unnecessarily, fabricates stories, and becomes upset. It cannot think of doing anything without expectation.

When I was in college, one day, I went to a shop to buy a book. There, I saw a beautifully wrapped chocolate. I thought of giving it to Amma. The day before, I had seen her relishing a chocolate that a devotee offered her. Excited by the prospect of Amma accepting my chocolate offering, I started fantasizing about how she would look at me, smile, and ask me where I got it from...

Though there were two other brahmacharini friends with me in the shop, I did not disclose my plans to them. I bought the chocolate secretly and kept it in my bag. If I had told them that it was for Amma, they would have been happy. But I selfishly wanted Amma's attention all for myself.

The next day, when Amma was giving darshan for ashram residents, I gave her the chocolate. She took it and kept it aside without even looking at it. This was not what I had expected! I was upset. Later, after reflecting on the matter, I realized that, the other day, Amma had been relishing not the chocolate but the devotee's love. I thought that I, too, was offering my chocolate with love, but my offering had been tainted by selfishness and expectation.

Expectation causes misery if we do not get what we want. Therefore, to be happy, we should drop our expectations. Lord Krishna says, *"Yogastha kuru karmani sangam tyaktva"*—"Remain steadfast and perform your duties, abandoning all attachment to the results" (*Bhagavad Gita*, 2.48). This means doing actions with full awareness, leaving aside our expectation of results. This is the attitude of a *karma yogi*. An action performed with expectation of results binds, whereas the same action done with the proper attitude leads to spiritual liberation.

A story that Amma tells makes this point clearer. Once, a man consumed a lot of ghee at a feast. The next day, his stomach became upset and he went to a doctor, who asked him to take a liter of ghee. Hearing this, the patient explained that eating too much ghee had caused indigestion, and therefore, he did not want more ghee. The doctor mixed a few ayurvedic herbs into the ghee, prescribed the dosage the patient needed to take, and dismissed him. The man took the medicine as prescribed and was cured.

Ghee, eaten in excess, made the man sick. The same ghee, when taken as medicine, healed him. Similarly, the same action can bind or liberate, depending on our attitude.

Mahatmas (spiritually illumined souls) like Amma always set the right example. She does every action with utmost concentration and awareness. When she serves lunch prasad, she does so amazingly fast. Even with four or five food serving lines, it is hard to keep up with Amma. Though she passes the plates rapidly, Amma looks at every person who comes to her and checks to see if each plate has sufficient rice and other items. It is usually Amma who notices the missing pickle in one plate, for example. When she has finished serving the prasad, Amma calculates how much time it took to serve *x* number of people. Watching her, it is clear that everything she does is optimal: maximum work done perfectly in the minimum time. Lord Krishna says, *'yogah karmasu kaushalam'*—'yoga is skill in action' (*Bhagavad Gita*, 2.50).

Once many years ago, when Amma came to the press, she noticed that the printing machine was dusty. This negligence made her sad. Amma wiped the machine with her own hands and said that we should see work as worship. She also said that just as we clean our prayer room before starting our worship, we should also clean our workplace and pray before starting work. If work is worship, its outcome is prasad. If we accept the results of our actions as prasad, we will remain equanimous whether we succeed or fail. This is what Lord Krishna meant when He said, *"Siddhyasiddyoh samo bhutva"*—"Remain even-minded in success and failure" (*Bhagavad Gita*, 2.48).

Failures are more instructive than successes. The pain of failing makes us stop and reflect on the real nature of things and their importance in our lives. This brings about personal transformation and improvement.

In 2019, India launched Chandrayaan-2, the country's second lunar exploration mission. The ISRO (Indian Space Research Organization) had worked hard for years to make this mission a success. However, just before Chandrayaan-2 was about to reach its goal, the lander crashed. Though the team was crestfallen, it accepted and learnt from the failure, and is now gearing up for Chandrayaan-3.

Just as failure can teach us important lessons, sadness can take us closer to God. When we are sad, our prayers are more heartfelt. That is why Kunti, the mother of the Pandavas (in the *Mahabharata*), always prayed to Lord Krishna for sorrows. She knew they would take her closer to him.

All of us have had experiences when we were sad and cried out to Amma. Let me share one such experience. I first met Amma when she came to Mumbai in 1987 for the first time. I was in sixth grade then. Amma had two programs daily for about two weeks. When she came to Mumbai next, Amma held programs for a month. She stayed in a house next to my parents' flat in Mumbai for more than 20 days. On most days, as Amma left the house for public programs, I would stand next to her car. Seeing me, Amma would ask, "Aren't you coming for the program?" Then she would take me along with her! When I was sleepy, she would put me in her lap. So, I would be with Amma the whole day. When I was not with Amma, I would go to the swamis to hear Amma's stories. One month passed in this way. When the programs ended and Amma was about to leave, I became heartbroken. It was difficult for me to stay away from Amma, but I had to go back to school.

After a few months, the dates for Amma's Kolkata program were announced. My parents decided to attend the program and asked one of Amma's devotees to look after me while they were away. I could not go as I had classes. After they left, I became sad. I missed Amma and would cry often. I had no spiritual knowledge but had become attached to Amma. I wanted only to see her and be with her.

After two days, Amma appeared in my dream. Holding a handful of her hairbands, she told me, "I'm sending these to you." When I woke up, I was thrilled as I had seen Amma and because she had said that she would send me her hairbands. I was sure that the dream would come true and eagerly waited for my parents to return. In those days, there were no mobile phones, and so, I could not call my mother to tell her about the dream.

In Kolkata, when Amma's program ended and she was about to leave, she called my mother, gave her a handful of her hairbands, and told her to give them to me. When my mother returned, she brought Amma's hairbands for me. I was overjoyed! What I saw in my dream came true.

Amma knows all our thoughts and sorrows and she is with us all the time. Then why should we worry? Let us work with an attitude of surrender to the Divine. When that attitude blossoms, we will enjoy peace and contentment. ☙

13

Openness of Heart
Bri. Niramayamrita Chaitanya

The Kurukushetra War, which took place more than 5,000 years ago, is still being discussed. What is its relevance today? The battlefield of Kurukshetra is a metaphor for the mind. Amma says, "The fiercest war is that which goes on in our mind. If we win that battle, nothing can ever defeat us." Arrayed on one side are the smaller forces of virtuous thoughts, and on the other, is the larger army of unvirtuous thoughts. The Arjuna in us is bound to become dejected sooner or later, and feel like giving up. Fortunately, the same *Paramatma* (Supreme Consciousness), who took the form of Lord Krishna then, has incarnated as the Mother of the Universe. This avatar of love and compassion is with us to help us win the battle against our lower nature.

Lord Krishna tells Arjuna,

> *ashocyananvashocastvam prajnavadamshca bhashase*
> *gatasunagatasumshca nanushocanti panditah*

> You grieve for those one need not grieve for, and yet, you speak like a person of wisdom. The wise do not grieve for either the living or the dead. (*Bhagavad Gita*, 2.11)

A *jnani* (knower of the Truth) is always equanimous; he is not attached to anything. Look at the vast sky. It contains everything—the air, clouds, sun, moon, stars, galaxies and so on—but is not attached to anything.

Often, we misunderstand detachment to mean being impassive. What I learnt from Amma is that detachment is a state of mental balance; it is total equanimity. We can see this supreme state of detachment only in *mahatmas* (spiritually illumined souls) like Amma. She embraces everyone and showers love and compassion on each, without any expectation whatsoever. Her only concern is the uplift of all.

I remember a story that Amma narrated about true detachment. Once, a strong and beautiful horse walked into the stable of a horse breeder. No one knew where it came from. When the neighbors learnt about it, they came to congratulate the breeder. They commented on how lucky he was. The breeder didn't say anything. He just smiled.

After a few days, the horse disappeared. The neighbors expressed sorrow at the loss. The horse breeder just smiled. He didn't say anything.

After a week, that horse returned with a few horses, all strong and beautiful. The neighbors congratulated the breeder: "How lucky you are! Now you have a large stable of horses!"

The breeder smiled but remained silent.

A few days passed. His only son went riding on one of the new horses. He fell and broke his hands and legs. The neighbors expressed regret: "How unfortunate! Alas, your only son hurt himself badly!"

This time, the breeder said, "My son fell from the horse and broke his limbs. This is the truth. Time will tell if it is fortunate or unfortunate."

After a week, soldiers came to the village and enlisted all the able-bodied youngsters to serve in the army, as the kingdom had come under attack from an enemy. The neighbors commented, "How lucky the horse breeder is! Only his son evaded enlistment."

Such is life. It is full of unexpected joys and sorrows, good luck and bad luck. Our mind is like those villagers, constantly murmuring. Amma is trying to make us like the horse breeder: calm and wise. She points out that most people have a tendency to swing towards extremes, soaring like a bird when elated or sinking like a stone when despondent.

Like the seven colors in sunlight, consciousness encompasses seven virtues: love, peace, knowledge, strength, happiness, purity and tranquility. However, we mistakenly imagine that love, peace and happiness are in objects and people, when they are actually innate. Amma says that we ought to be like a *'tantedi.'* This Malayalam word is usually used to refer to someone who is bold and fearless. But Amma explains the word this way: *"tante idattil irikkuka"* (remain within oneself). A bhajan that Amma often sings explains how.

> *ullatonnum ullilallatilla mattengum*
> *atu kanditanay ullinullil cellanam nammal*

That which truly exists is in us. To see it, we must turn within.

In the *Bhagavad Gita*, Lord Krishna tells a grieving Arjuna that all those he is grieving for are not the ephemeral body but the eternal consciousness. Most of the sorrows we feel are also over transient matters. Separation from Amma also causes us pain. When I was sent to do seva at the Tanur Amrita Vidyalayam (AV), I went for darshan. Whenever I go for darshan, I would note points down on a piece of paper. That day I had written: "Amma, I want to see you like this always. Even when I am in

Tanur, I want to see you the way I see you now. Amma, please come with me!"

Amma read the note and laughed. Then she said, "You should embrace the pillars and coconut trees there and, forgetting everything else, call out to Amma. I was also like that."

When I heard this, I happily left for Tanur. On reaching the school, I looked at each of the coconut trees. I thought, if I embrace the trees now, what would the children, teachers and parents think? They might wonder, "What happened to madam? She was fine until yesterday." So, I told myself, "Not now" and went to my room.

That evening, I went to the verandah as usual to do *japa* (repeated chanting of the mantra). Everyone had left and I was alone. After my japa, I took a good look at the pillars. Then I went running to them and hugged them tightly, calling out loudly, "Amma! Amma!"

The sharp edges of the pillars pressed painfully into my body. I could not feel the softness, coolness or fragrance of Amma's body, or the bliss we get when she kisses us. I thought, "Amma tricked me," and slowly walked back to my room. Later, I thought, "Amma won't say anything meaningless. It is because of my limited understanding that I have failed to understand her words."

In the *Bhagavad Gita*, Lord Krishna says,

raso'hamapsu kaunteya prabhasmi shashisuryayoh
pranavah sarvavedeshu shabdah khe paurusham nrshu

O Arjuna, I am the taste in water, the radiance of the sun and moon, the syllable 'Om' in the Vedas, the sound in ether, and virility in men. (7.8)

Maybe Amma was trying to tell me to see her as the quintessence of each and every thing. Another important teaching, one that she always stresses, is *shraddha* (attentiveness). The truth though is that however careful we may be, the actions of others can also create problems in our life. To illustrate, Amma says that even if we drive carefully, another driver who is careless can ram his car into ours and hurt us. I am reminded of an incident that happened in the Tanur AV in 2010.

After a student, who was the son of a senior teacher in our school, passed his 10th grade examinations, he applied for admission to the 11th and 12th grades in our school. When his 10th grade certificate arrived, we saw that his date of birth was wrong. The staff who entered the details online had made a mistake. To rectify the error, we had to contact the CBSE (Central Board of Secondary Education) Office in Chennai, and the whole process would take a long time.

I got caught up with work and forgot to follow it up. The student sat for both the 12th grade and college entrance examinations, both of which he passed. He also gained admission to a computer engineering degree course in a college near his house. However, as his 10th grade certificate was not in order, the college gave him temporary admission. He was to produce the correct certificate within 15 days, failing which his admission would be cancelled.

I became tense. The principal of AV Ernakulam, Swamini Bhaktipriyamrita, helped me a lot. She asked the principal of Chennai AV to go to the CBSE office and check if the correction had been made. She also obtained the CBSE secretary's number, which she passed to me. I started calling him daily. After a few days, he got irritated with me and told me that he did not like being bothered persistently (especially on his personal phone).

Ten days passed. The 11th day was a Saturday. The student's mother came to me and warned me that her husband was upset.

She said that he used to be in the army, and was blaming her for jeopardizing their son's future by enrolling him in AV.

I did not say anything but looked at Amma's photo, mentally beseeching her for help. The next day was Sunday. I spent the whole day praying to Amma: "O Amma, the school's reputation is at stake. People will say that we ruined the boy's future owing to our negligence. Amma, he's a good boy. Please help him."

On Monday, when the couriers came, I ran to them... but there was nothing. That evening, the boy's mother came to me and said, "My husband will be coming here tomorrow. Madam, please don't blame me if he speaks to you roughly."

The image of a drunken soldier sporting a handlebar moustache rose in my mind. I was so scared that I could not sleep that night.

Tuesday morning dawned. I thought, "If he doesn't get that certificate today, his admission will be cancelled tomorrow." I decided to call the CBSE secretary. I thought it was the day of my doom anyway. So what if shouts at me over the phone? I called him. He picked up the phone. Before I could speak, he said, "Madam, I have sent the corrected certificate. You will get it today."

I had no words to express my joy. I ran to the puja room and thanked Amma profusely. I arranged with the Post Office to send the certificate to the teacher as soon as possible.

That night, her husband called me to thank me. He said, "Madam, I have regained my faith in Amma. It is only because of Amma's power that we obtained the certificate today."

The next day, he and his family members came to the school. They made offerings of oil, wicks, incense sticks, big packets of almonds, pistachios and cashew nuts, pens and bed linen at the altar to Amma.

In the first week of August, after Amma had returned from her Summer Tour, I went for darshan with this note and a packet of almonds: "O Amma, by your infinite grace, that boy's certificate came on time. To express their happiness, his family brought almonds, pistachios, cashew nuts, pens and a bed sheet. I took the pens. I placed the pistachios and cashew nuts in front of your photo during the puja. After the puja, I ate them. The bed sheet is waiting in Tanur for your arrival. This packet of almonds is for you!"

Amma read it aloud and burst out laughing. She then ate a few almonds. When Amma came to Tanur in 2014, she stayed in our school and used the bed on which that bedsheet had been spread.

This incident taught me that one careless mistake on our part can affect others. In this instance, Amma's grace alone saved us.

Let me narrate how we (my two older sisters and I) came to join the ashram. In December 1986, Amma had a program at the Moothakunnam Siva Temple. I was in 8th grade. As I had exams, I could not go to the temple. After the temple program, Amma visited two houses near our home. We saw Amma for the first time in one of those houses. To our knowledge, the members of that family have not gone to see Amma even once after that. Therefore, we still believe that Amma actually went there to see us!

Our parents would take us to see Amma whenever she visited places nearby. They also bought Amma's photos and many bhajan cassettes for us. After one or two darshans, we wanted to see Amma again and again, and we spent long hours listening to her bhajans. When he saw the changes in us, father's attitude changed. He took away the cassettes and photos. We were strictly forbidden from going to see Amma. As a result, we started seeing her without his knowledge.

Father was working outside Kerala, and would come home only once or twice a year. When he was away, we used to pester our mother to let us see Amma; we even went without her knowledge. Sometimes, we would say that we had extra classes or tuition. Mother would say that she was going to visit relatives. Often, we would meet each other in the queue for Amma's darshan! Even though we would lie to see Amma, she would receive us as if she had been waiting for a long time to see us. Every time, she would say, "O, my daughters have come!"

Once, we heard that Amma was going to inaugurate the temple in the Kaloor Ashram. As father was not home, we pestered mother until she gave in. We wanted to eat before leaving. But when we asked mother for food, she said, "I'm not your mother, am I? *Your* mother will give you food!"

Hearing this, we also became obstinate and left without eating. We reached Kaloor. After the program and darshan ended, Amma went to her room. We waited downstairs. Our plan was to leave after Amma left. By that time, we were terribly hungry. Suddenly, Bri. Leelavati (now Swamini Matrupriya) came to us and asked, "Why do all of you look so pale? Are you tired? Come, let's go up. There is food for us there."

She took us upstairs. There, we enjoyed a lavish feast with two kinds of *payasam* (sweet pudding)!

When we returned home, we triumphantly told mother, "Amma gave us a feast with two kinds of payasam!"

Even though our parents initially resisted our joining the ashram, eventually, they came around.

In 2005, our mother was diagnosed with third stage uterine cancer. It was an unbearable blow for father and our sister at home.

The doctors ruled out surgery but prescribed 24 rounds of radiation and chemotherapy. Whenever my mother or sister called, I would try to console and infuse confidence in them by telling them stories Amma told us, including the story of the horse trader. I would also visualize Amma sitting near mother and caressing her head and the cancer-ridden parts of her body. Whenever I felt sad, I would resort to this visualization and get some relief.

The treatment started. Although I would inquire how mother was doing, I never asked about radiation or hair loss, which is usually an inevitable side effect. On the last day of her treatment, we went to see her in AIMS Hospital. I imagined that she would be in a pitiable condition and decided that I would not reveal my anguish.

To my surprise, mother was in good shape. There was no hair loss or radiation scars! I felt that Amma must have caressed my mother during her treatment, just as I had visualized. More than 15 years have passed, and mother is still alive, healthy and happy. A million thanks to Amma for her infinite blessings!

To make life meaningful, we should become a tool in Amma's hands. We should see bitter experiences as opportunities to learn valuable lessons. We may make mistakes, but we should be able to correct them and move ahead. Most importantly, we should be able to open our heart fully before Amma. Whatever crisis we face, let us hold on tightly to her holy feet. May Amma bless us with all these qualities. ☺☙

14

Surrender
Br. Mukundamrita Chaitanya

The *Bhagavad Gita* explains succinctly how one may gain Self-knowledge.

> *tadviddhi pranipatena pariprashnena sevaya*
> *upadekshyanti te jnanam jnaninastatva-darshinah*

> By humbly submitting to the wise, by asking them questions, and by serving them, they, who have realized the Truth, will impart wisdom to you. (4.34)

The *Mundakopanishad* hints at the fullness of Self-knowledge:

> *kasmin nu bhagavo vijnate sarvam idam vijnatam bhavati iti.*

> What is that, knowing which, everything becomes known? (1.1.13)

Lord Krishna also declares,

> *na hi jnanena sadrsham pavitramiha vidyate*

> In this world, there is nothing as purifying as divine knowledge. (*Bhagavad Gita*, 4.38)

The Guru imparts knowledge that cannot be taught. Through silence, she imparts what cannot be explained by words. Only a disciple who is humble, dedicated and surrendered can receive this knowledge. To awaken that knowledge, the disciple should have an inner tuning with the Guru. In the *Mahabharata*, Ekalavya learnt archery from his master Dronacharya in this way. He made an idol of his Guru, worshipped it, and was able to master all the intricacies and techniques of archery without even once interacting physically with his master. If we truly love our Guru, all knowledge will flow into us. If we have humility, dedication and purity, we will receive the Guru's grace. A toddler is surrendered to its mother; it understands that it can do nothing without its mother's help. What the Guru does is to shatter the false notion that we can accomplish certain things through our skill. She helps us realize that we can do nothing by our will alone.

Anything of the external world can be taught and learned. But only a Guru can bestow knowledge of eternity. The Guru does so in silence; through long contemplation and meditation, the disciple understands her teachings.

When a spiritual master was asked who his relatives were, he said,

satyam mata pita jnanam dharmo bhrata daya sakha
shantih patni kshama putrah shadete mama bandhavah

Truth is my mother, knowledge is my father, righteousness is my brother, mercy is my friend, calmness (peacefulness) is my wife, and forgiveness, my son. These six are my near and dear ones.

These are also the qualities that a spiritual aspirant must cultivate. Divine knowledge dawns only in righteous hearts. The disciple should be humble enough so that the river of knowledge flowing from the Guru reaches him. More than physically prostrating before her, what matters is the state of a disciple's mind; that is the truest offering at the Guru's feet.

The disciple can tap into the wisdom of the Guru through humble queries. From the question, the Guru can understand the disciple's state of mind. She can then remove the disciple's negativities and lead him to the right path. That is why many of the Hindu scriptural texts are in the form of dialogues between master and disciple. Gradually, the disciple becomes elevated to the Guru's plane.

Years ago, an engineering graduate asked Amma, "Is there a God?"

Amma replied, "It is like asking (with the use of one's tongue) whether the tongue exists. Son, what is it that you seek?"

The young man replied, "If there is a God, I'm so angry with him that I want to kill him!"

"Why?" asked Amma.

"In this world, millions of people are suffering from disease and poverty while others enjoy good health and wealth. Every being in the creation is food for another in the food chain. How cruel the world is! I'm so angry with God, whose creation is so cruel, that I want to kill him!"

Amma said, "Amma likes you very much. You are not angry with God for selfish reasons but because of compassion for others. God doesn't punish anyone. It is we who punish ourselves. It is the wrong thoughts we have and wrong actions we do that come back to us as bad karma. Every action has an equivalent reaction."

The young man's next question was, "Are you God?"

Amma replied, "I'm a crazy girl! I'm here because nobody has put me in jail. Amma is not saying that you should believe in God or Amma. It's enough if you believe in yourself."

Like a tree lying dormant inside a seed, there is divine consciousness in every sentient and insentient object of the universe. With the right knowledge, prayers, actions and thoughts, we can uplift ourselves to the state of the divine. Through *sadhana* (spiritual practices) and with the Guru's grace, we can awaken our divine qualities. God incarnates to help us do so.

When the young man who asked the questions realized that Amma was the personification of infinite divine virtues, he joined her ashram. The young man later became Swami Purnamritananda Puri.

Seva is not just physical work. Truly serving the master means living according to her teachings and striving sincerely to bring about a change in ourselves.

After attaining enlightenment, the Buddha attracted many followers, including many of his relatives. One of them was Ananda, the Buddha's first cousin. Ananda told the Buddha, "Lord, I have one prayer: I want to be with you and serve you all the time. I will take care of all your needs."

The Buddha agreed but said, "You shouldn't impose any condition on your Guru. Doing so will obstruct your spiritual growth." Thereafter, Ananda was always with the Buddha. By the Lord's grace, many disciples attained Self-realization. Ananda was witness to this as he was always with him.

One day, a 17-year-old disciple who had started to live with the Buddha just a year before attained *bhava samadhi*, a state of devotional ecstasy. Seeing this, Ananda was shattered. He fell at the Buddha's feet and cried. "Oh Lord, this kid came barely a year ago, and he has attained that divine state. Many others have also attained that state by your grace. I've been with you every moment of the day for 46 years. Why haven't I received even a taste of that divine state?"

The Buddha smiled and said, "Dear Ananda, you were only looking after my physical body. You did not assimilate any of my teachings. You thought of me as this body. You thought gaining that spiritual state was a kind of barter. I attained that state through my own effort and inquiry. You, too, can attain that state in a similar way."

He continued, "Become a light unto yourself. You will understand the truth if you surrender to the light within. It is the light of knowledge. It is the true nature of all beings. It is the light of all lights."

Amma has blessed us all with different divine experiences at some point in our lives. I first met Amma in Kodungallur in 1988 during the Brahmasthanam Temple festival there. After that, I started visiting Amritapuri regularly. In 1992, I joined Amritha ITC (Industrial Training Centre) in Puthiyakavu as a teacher. In 1995, by Amma's grace, I joined the ashram. Amma asked me to do seva in the printing press. I serviced and maintained all the machines with Br. Babu (now Swami Dharmamritananda). He took care of the mechanical section whereas I took care of the machines' electrical and electronic parts.

One morning after archana, Br. Sreekumar (now Swami Gurupadasritananda) asked me to go to the press immediately as the cutting machine was not working. There were only two days left for the next posting of the *Matruvani* magazines, and this was the only cutting machine. When I turned on the machine, I heard strange sounds coming from the machine's motherboard. As the machine was made and programmed in Japan, I was not sure how to repair it. If we called a professional service engineer, we would have to wait for at least a week. The service fee would also be astronomical. I spent the whole day fruitlessly trying to figure out what the problem was. All those who were helping me went for the evening bhajans. Feeling totally helpless, I prayed to Amma, "What should I do Amma? I have failed to solve the problem."

Suddenly, Amma walked into the press! She asked, "Son, are you here alone? What happened to the machine?" I explained all that had happened. She peered into the machine, and said, "It's full of dust." Amma wiped something on the motherboard. Then, gently patting my chest, she said, "Don't worry, son. Try again. It will become all right." Saying so, she walked away.

Amma's words and touch infused new energy and enthusiasm in me. I sat silently for a while. Then a thought came to mind. Why did Amma touch just one board when there were 18 similar ones in the machine? I decided to focus on the board that Amma had touched. Although it was difficult to dismantle it, I somehow managed to do so. When I checked it, I saw, to my surprise, that there was a contact missing on the board. I rectified it and the machine started working! With just one glance, Amma had figured out what I had not been able to, even after eight hours of hard work. That evening, I realized the truth of what Amma often says: that what crowns effort with success is divine grace.

The next day, I went to Amma and told her that the machine was working. Acting as if she did not know anything, she asked, "What was the problem?"

I answered, "What Amma indicated was the problem."

Amma smiled and said, "I just looked over the machine, that's all."

If we try to do our work sincerely, dedicating all that we do to Amma, she will always help us; that is what I learnt from this incident. May she always act through us. May her grace protect us all. ৩ৡৢ

15

Shraddha
Br. Keertanamrita Chaitanya

Perhaps the most salient among Amma's teachings is *shraddha* (awareness). Amma says, "We should have awareness in every word we utter, every action we perform, and every thought we think. Most people spend their entire lives thinking about what happened in their past and worrying about the future. Their minds are scattered. As a result, they are unable to focus their attention on anything they do, and thereby end up losers, instead of being victorious."

Amma frequently speaks about how her mother, Damayanti-amma, used to discipline her during her childhood. "While husking rice, Damayanti-amma would not allow even a single grain to fall out. She would say that we must value the efforts of the paddy farmer." One instruction that Amma gives is, "The washed pots should be cleaned so well that they ought to reflect our faces, like a mirror. We should have such awareness and fastidiousness in every action we do."

Shraddha also means faith, especially faith in the Guru and her words. Lord Krishna says,

shraddhavan labhate jnanam tatparah samyatendriyah
jnanam labdhva param shantim acirenadhigacchati

One who has full faith, devotion and control over his senses attains knowledge. Having attained it, he soon attains everlasting peace. (*Bhagavad Gita*, 4.39)

This verse highlights three qualities needed to make progress in spiritual life: shraddha (faith), *tatparah* (devotion) and *indriya samyamana* (sense control). In *Vivekachudamani* ('Crown Jewel of Discernment'), Sri Shankaracharya defines shraddha in this way:

shastrasya guruvakyasya satyabuddhyavadharanam
sa shraddha kathita sadbhiryaya vastupalabhyate

Shraddha is the conviction that the scriptures and Guru's teachings are true. It is the means by which Reality is known. (25)

To learn about anything, one needs a teacher. This holds true for the spiritual life, too. One who knows the ultimate truth is a *jnani*. One who leads a seeker to it is a Guru. '*Gu*' denotes darkness and '*ru*' denotes light. The Guru dispels the darkness of ignorance and leads us to the light of wisdom.

Once a disciple approached a Guru and asked him how to find God. The Guru said, "I will show you how. I will draw a picture of a person. If you can find the person in the picture, you can see God in him."

The Guru drew a picture and gave it to the disciple, who searched many places for that person. Failing to find him, he returned to the Guru and told him that he could not find the person. The Guru drew another picture and gave it to the disciple, who went out in search again. This time, too, he failed. This continued many times. Finally, the disciple became fed up and said, "O Guru, I've searched high and low but I still haven't found even one of the people you drew. You've been fooling me! I really want to see God. Please show me how."

Hearing this, the Guru said, "All right, I shall. Sit here." The Guru then drew a portrait of the disciple. Seeing this, the disciple exclaimed, "But this is me!"

The Guru replied, "Yes, it is. God, whom you seek, resides in you. All you need to do is realize it."

When we are sick, we consult a doctor, and take the medicines that he or she prescribes. Our faith in the doctor and obedience in taking the prescribed medicines heal us. Similarly, to heal *bhava roga*, the disease of worldliness, we must resort to and obey a Guru. Faith in the Guru takes us to the light of spiritual wisdom.

Lord Krishna says that there are three types of shraddha:

trividha bhavati shraddha dehinam sa svabhavaja
sattviki rajasi caiva tamasi ceti tam shrnu

Every human being is born with innate faith, which is of three kinds — *sattvic* (pure), *rajasic* (passionate) and *tamasic* (dull). (*Bhagavad Gita*, 17.2)

It is sattvic faith that takes one to God. Developing that faith is a matter of evolution. Amma sings about it in *'Oru nimisham enkilum.' 'krimiyay puzhuvay izhayunna jantukkal palatay paravakal mrgavumayi...'* — "Having evolved through various forms like the worm, slithering creatures, birds and beasts..."

A human birth, the crème de la crème of evolution, is priceless. Whereas all other living beings live according to their primal tendencies, humans alone have the faculty of discernment. Only we can distinguish between virtue (which gives *punya*) and vice (*papa*). The transition from the human to the divine requires us to cross the ocean of *samsara* (worldliness). Left to ourselves, we

will drown. But there is a boat that can take us across. All that we
need to do is to get into the boat and sit quietly. The boatwoman
is the Guru, and she will take us across.

Once during a flight, just before the airplane was about to land,
the weather suddenly became turbulent. The pilot announced,
"Please fasten your seatbelts!"

The passengers became frightened. One passenger noticed
a boy sitting near him. He was looking out of the window and
seemed relaxed and not in the least bit frightened. After some
time, the pilot somehow managed to land. The other passenger
asked the boy, "Weren't you scared?"

The boy smiled and said, "No. The captain is my father. I knew
that he would land safely without causing me any harm."

We should be like this boy; we should have the faith that
whatever the problem, our Guru will take care of us. If we have
this attitude, we will never fear or falter in any circumstance.

During a concert, the singer tests her *shruti* (pitch) against a
tamburu (drone). In the same way, what bestows harmony in the
life of a seeker is tuning into and obeying the Guru's teachings.

Music brought me closer to Amma. I have been fortunate
enough to play the *tabla* (Indian hand drums) for her on many
occasions.

Once before I joined the ashram, while I was still a student,
I accompanied my tabla teacher to the recording studio of
Devarajan Master, a renowned composer. Back then, studio
technology was such that everything—the orchestral music and
singing—was recorded together. If anyone made a mistake, the
whole song would have to be rerecorded. Hence, it was vital that
everyone was attentive. Devarajan Master was a stern taskmaster
who inspired fear and reverence in equal measure in the musicians.
As a result, most of his songs would be recorded in a single take.
I still remember seeing the musicians sitting in the studio with

utmost shraddha and humility. Many of them became famous later. No doubt, their attentiveness and receptivity elevated them.

I received a similar training when I started to play the tabla during Amma's recording sessions. Recording with her is truly intense. Before she arrives, the singers and instrumentalists are supposed to practice the song(s). After Amma arrives, she will decide which song(s) she wants to record. We must be completely focused. During the recording, she might want one particular line to be repeated many times. No one can predict how many iterations Amma wants or when she will move to the next line. Often, the indication to start the next line comes at the last moment, and the instrumentalist has to be ready to make the transition immediately.

Amma says, "I am not a singer." But her flair for and knowledge of music are stupendous. I have never seen any other singer sing in so many languages and tunes. Her power of recall is also perfect. Years after Amma has recorded a song, she will render it perfectly. Often, the other musicians would have forgotten the tune, but not Amma. This is indicative of Amma's perfect shraddha.

Once, I had an opportunity to meet many celebrated singers. My friends introduced me to them as a brahmachari who plays the tabla for Amma. They were keen to learn about Amma's bhajans and how they are recorded. When I shared my experiences with them, they were surprised because though they are professionals, they practice thoroughly before recording a song. As far as they were concerned, only someone with an extraordinary grasp and awareness can learn and record songs in a single take. They said, "Amma is the very deity of awareness!" Hearing this, I felt great pride. I consider being able to play the tabla for Amma one of the biggest blessings in my life.

Apart from playing the tabla, Amma also assigned me the responsibility of managing the students' canteen in the Mysore campus of Amrita University. Here, too, I continue to receive training in awareness. One of my colleagues is a hard working brahmacharini. Seeing her work often makes me feel guilty for not working as hard. Once I told her, "Sister, we have many workers. You don't need to work so hard!" But she did not pay any heed to my words. Finally, I told Amma about this. She said, "She is such a self-sacrificing soul!" When I heard this, I felt jealous and told Amma, "I, too, work very hard!" Amma smiled and said, "Good! It will help you reduce your belly!" She continued, "A brahmachari should never be lazy and unaware. He should always be aware and awake." From then on, I began applying myself more diligently in the kitchen.

After a while, I felt that I had learnt everything that needed to be learnt and that I could manage everything single-handedly. At this time, Amma came to Kannur for programs. While playing the tabla for Swamiji (Swami Amritaswarupananda), I received a message on my phone. There were some food-related problems at the Mysore campus. Minutes later, Amma, who was giving darshan, called me to her side. She had learnt that Health Inspectors were going to the Mysore campus for an inspection and asked me to go there immediately. I told Amma, "Amma, I'm scared. I don't want to go back."

Amma pacified me. "Son, don't be afraid. Go there coura-geously. Just go there for a day. You can come to the next program in Palakkad. That brahmacharini is all alone." When I heard this, I felt upset, thinking that Amma was concerned only about the brahmacharini.

I reached Mysore early the next morning. Three inspectors came from the Health Department. One of them said, "This is Amma's institution. We know there won't be any problem here." But another inspector insisted on checking everything. They checked every nook and corner of the kitchen, but could not find anything amiss. Finally, they said, "We apologize for troubling you," and left. Only then did I appreciate what Amma meant when she said that I could attend the next program.

I first saw Amma when I was in 9th grade. I was supposed to participate in the tabla competition of the School Youth Festival as a representative of the Kozhikode District. My father, a devotee of Amma, took me to her Kozhikode program to get her blessings. When I went for darshan, Amma gave me *rava laddu* (sweet semolina ball) as prasad. When I saw that Amma gave sweets to others, I took my prasad as a special blessing. That year, I won second prize in the tabla competition.

Even before I went to college, tabla playing became my profession. I began to receive invitations to play for various concerts, and slowly my ways began to change. I picked up bad habits. In a bid to make me give them up, my parents forcibly sent me to Mysore to help my elder brother in his business. There, we both enrolled for a diploma program. In this college, I met many musicians. I started hanging around with them and played for concerts with them. In no time at all, I resumed my bad habits.

At this juncture, I received an invitation to play the tabla for a program at the Sri Ramakrishna Math. There, I learnt about *mahatmas* (spiritually illumined souls), Gurus and sannyasis. (Even though I had met Amma, I did not know much about her or her ashram.) Slowly, I became close to the monks of the Ramakrishna Math. Because of their influence, my bad habits dropped away, one by one.

During this time, while traveling through Mysore City one day, I saw a poster announcing Amma's visit to Mysore. I recalled my previous darshan and decided to see her. When I went for darshan, I was so captivated by her and just knew that she was my

Guru. Thereafter, I started going to the Mysore Ashram regularly. I also started visiting Amritapuri frequently.

It was during this phase that a continuous fever began to trouble me. Although I consulted many doctors, my condition did not improve; in fact, it became worse. I told Amma about this and she asked me to go to AIMS Hospital immediately. There, the doctors discovered that the problem was my lungs, a problem created by my own past bad habits. The doctors advised immediate surgery.

Unfortunately, I did not have enough money for the surgery. Amma's ashram in Mysore promised to help me get a concession from AIMS. In the meantime, I visited Amritapuri again for Amma's darshan. At that time, I noticed her talking to two brahmacharinis but did not hear what she told them. After leaving Amritapuri, I went back home to try and borrow money from friends and relatives for the operation, as my parents did not have enough. My parents consoled me, saying that Amma would definitely help.

At that time, a friend promised to pay for all the expenses. However, knowing my nature, he said that he would not give me any money but would pay the hospital directly. I was admitted to AIMS and my surgery was carried out successfully. The day I was supposed to be discharged, my friend who was with me was asked to contact the Patient Services department. There, Bri. Rahana, the person in charge of the department, asked him why we had not informed them about my surgery. She said that Amma had personally instructed her not to charge us even a penny. Surprised, my friend rushed to inform me about what Amma had said. When I heard this, I could not control my emotions. I started sobbing. Hearing my cries, the nurses came running and asked what the problem was. They said that patients are usually happy at the time of their discharge. I explained that I had been so moved by Amma's compassion that I could not help crying. I also realized that Amma had redeemed my parents' faith in and devotion to her.

When I went to AIMS for a follow-up, the doctors asked me about my profession. I said I was a tabla player. They advised me to reduce my playing as it may adversely affect my lungs. When I told Amma what the doctors advised, she asked me to remain in the Mysore Ashram and to continue my tabla practice there.

Recently, during a recording of 'Omkara Divya Porule,' I played for more than three hours continuously. It is only by her grace that I was able to play like this. Over and over again, I have come to understand the importance of a Guru in one's life. May Amma's grace help us all progress on the spiritual path. ♋

16

Even-mindedness

Bri. Ameyamrita Chaitanya

What is yoga? It is that which unites.

What is the difference between normal exercises and *hatha yoga*? From an external viewpoint, hatha yoga is seen as certain physical postures. But the major difference between it and other forms of exercise is that yoga aims to elevate the mind to a state of total awareness by uniting physical movements with the body's breathing movements. So, at the gross level, yoga is union of the mind, body and *prana* (vital breath).

There are other definitions of yoga. The *Bhagavad Gita* offers several definitions. One of them is found in the following verse:

> *yogasthah kuru karmani sangam tyaktva dhananjaya*
> *siddhyasiddhyoh samo bhutva samatvam yoga ucyate*
>
> Remaining steadfast in yoga, O Arjuna, perform actions, abandoning attachment and remaining balanced in success and failure. This evenness of mind is called yoga. (2.48)

Here, yoga is defined as equanimity of mind.

What then is *karma yoga*? Any action is *karma*. When the karma unites the doer with God, karma becomes karma yoga. This is what Lord Krishna explains in the *Bhagavad Gita*.

In Amma's own words, "There was a time when people used to strew my path with thorns. Now, people shower flowers. In all situations, I remain as That. I have always been one with the One."

Being 'one with the One' — only *mahatmas* (spiritually illumined souls) like Amma always dwell in this supreme state of yoga.

Lord Sri Krishna explains to Arjuna how actions need to be performed, and what attitude he needs to have towards both the action and its fruit. He stresses detachment (*sangam tyaktva*) and an attitude of even-mindedness towards success and failure (*siddhyasiddhyoh samo bhutva*).

Amma explains the same principle in simple yet practical ways:

- Work is worship.
- Say yes to life.
- Live in the present.
- Move forward with self-confidence.
- Happiness is a decision.
- Everything is the will of God.
- Both grace and self-effort are important.
- If you become a zero, then you can become a hero.

We get innumerable opportunities to practice *samatva* (equanimity), especially in the presence of a master like Amma. The seva that Amma assigns to us plays a vital role in bringing about equanimity and surrender. Eventually, they just happen by her grace.

When I joined the ashram, I dreamt of a life in Amma's physical presence. But after just a month, I was asked to teach in Amrita Vidyalayam. I obeyed, albeit unwillingly. But I had the faith that Amma would always be with me.

Three years passed. One day, I was asked to take charge of Amrita Vidyalayam, Trivandrum. I had no choice but to obey Amma's words and accept the situation.

I am still learning how to obey and accept. In order to gain true acceptance and surrender, we should give up our likes and dislikes. This is not easy. But Amma puts us in situations where we learn to forgo our likes and dislikes, and to focus only on obeying and pleasing her.

Amma says, "The ego is the cause of desires and expectations." The ego makes us think that we are the doers. It also makes us hope that the outcome of our efforts will be to our liking. But when it is not, we deem it a failure and become upset.

One can act with total detachment and without concern for any particular outcome only when one has no ego. Only mahatmas like Amma are totally egoless. That is why every action she does is beautiful and perfect, and why the outcome is always favorable.

There are many instances that show how Amma accepts every situation and moves forward fearlessly. One example was the 2004 tsunami. As soon as the temporary needs of the survivors were arranged, Amma's next focus was on providing permanent homes for those who had lost theirs in the disaster.

When the construction of the houses was about to start, most of the ashram residents and many other volunteers were raring to help. Our enthusiasm and energy knew no bounds. But Amma sounded a note of caution: "I want all of you to promise me that no matter what comments you hear during the construction, you will not react. Accept the comments silently. Some may shower praises and love on you; a few may criticize. Whatever it is, accept it silently, do your duty, and return."

Amma's words show how totally detached she is from the fruits of her actions. She just does what she sees as her *dharma* (duty), giving her 100% to it, with no expectation.

To help us to reach this state of detachment and mental equipoise, Amma asks us to perform all our actions with a worshipful attitude and to accept the outcome with *prasada buddhi*, i.e. as divine dispensation.

I am reminded of an incident that took place during a recent North Indian Tour. During the first lunch stop with Amma, a Western devotee asked, "Amma what should our attitude be during this tour? What attitude will please you?"

Amma's reply was precise and beautiful. "Accept every situation as prasad from Amma. When we go to a temple and receive prasad, we don't analyze its quantity, quality or taste. We just accept it with reverence. We should have the same attitude towards the various challenging situations we may encounter in the course of this tour."

This beautiful message was not relevant only to the tour; it was a message for life, too. In order to gain prasada buddhi, we need to work with a worshipful attitude. Only if we do work as if it were worship can we cultivate the sense that we are merely instruments in the hands of God. This will create in us a sense of detachment towards the work we do, which, in turn, will help us to accept the outcome as if it were a gift from God. This is the equanimity of mind that Lord Krishna glorifies as yoga.

I am reminded about an incident that happened after the 2001 earthquake in Gujarat. Amma visited Bhuj after the ashram had reconstructed three villages that had been badly affected. She asked the villagers if they were upset. Their reply was as follows: All that we had was from God. Now, he has taken it back. There is nothing to be upset about.

Hearing these words, Amma's face lit up. This is a striking example of the attitude of prasada buddhi.

Let me share an incident from my life. A few years ago, I was facing serious problems in the school. Under immense pressure, I rushed to Amma to unburden my heart. But as it often happens, I could not utter a single word during darshan. Amma held me for a long time as she spoke to somebody beside her. I mentally narrated all my problems to her. Finally, Amma released me. Gazing at me, she lovingly said, "You need muscles not only in your hands. You must develop the muscles of your heart as well. Know that you are not a meek lamb, but a lion cub. Face every situation that comes your way with a positive attitude."

Before darshan, I had been totally shaken and had turned to Amma in sheer helplessness. Her words filled my distressed heart with so much strength and energy that I returned to school with confidence. The very next day, things started falling in place automatically and all the problems were resolved without much effort on my part. Even though I did not directly tell Amma anything, knowing my mind, she consoled me and her grace saw me through.

When we perform an action, what matters most is how and with what attitude we act. These matter more than the result of the action. Amma performs each and every action with love. Amma has said that only if we love what we do can we give it our all. Once, Swami Ramakrishnananda asked Amma how she is always able to remain happy. Amma's answer was that, whatever she does, she does happily, with love and with her whole being. And as she is not bound by the results of her actions, she is always happy.

This might not be possible for ordinary human beings like us. That is why Amma also teaches us to celebrate our failures. She often narrates an incident that took place during an Olympics event several years ago. It was the last event: a marathon. Half way through the race, the athlete from Ethiopia fell and injured his leg badly. The other athletes continued running. When they reached the stadium, everyone started applauding. Long after the winner had crossed the line, to everyone's surprise, this hurt Ethiopian athlete entered the stadium, limping. He slowly ran with a bandaged leg to the finishing line. As he ran, the crowds gave him a standing ovation, almost as if he had been the real winner.

Reporters interviewing him asked him, "Was it not foolish on your part to inflict pain on yourself unnecessarily when you knew that you would not win?"

The athlete replied, "My country sent me here not just to start running but to finish as well."

Likewise, we might also encounter failures, but we should not be discouraged. Our focus should be on our goal.

During darshan, Amma often tells us, "My children, be happy." Sometimes, she asks, "Happy?" She often says that happiness is a decision. Whether we laugh or cry, time will pass. So why not choose to laugh and be happy instead of crying? So, when Amma asks, "Happy?" she is telling us to choose happiness as our abiding emotion. In order to remain happy all the time, we must be able to accept success and failure, pain and pleasure, with equanimity.

While interviewing a successful businessman, a journalist asked, "What is the secret behind your success?"

The businessman answered in two words: "Right decisions."

"How do you make right decisions?"

"Experience."

"How did you acquire such experience?"

"Wrong decisions."

So, it all depends on how we accept, understand and surrender to situations. Amma puts it beautifully: when we see a bud, we fail to recognize that it is the last stage of the transition to a flower. Inside the bud, there is darkness, but from that darkness, it slowly blossoms into the light.

Let us put forth the right effort with self-confidence. If we do so, we will ultimately be able to realize our true self. If our mind is filled with the light of Amma's love, all experiences, whether good or bad, will bring us happiness. We will be able to celebrate not only our success but also our failures.

By Amma's grace, may we be able to discharge all our duties with discernment and evenness of mind. ༄༅༄

17

Journey of a Lifetime
Swamini Samadamrita Prana

I was an ordinary girl from Mumbai: studious, ambitious and fun-loving. In 1989, children from my neighborhood were taken to see a 'Mataji' ('Holy Mother') from Kerala who gave hugs and candies. I watched Amma sing bhajans, but left before the program ended. My mother bought Amma's biography and books of teachings, and began sharing devotees' experiences with my brother and me. I soon became interested in Amma, and began attending every program. I was also attracted by the serene personalities of Amma's disciples. I no longer wanted to be a doctor, but one of those disciples. I started doing spiritual practices, reading Amma's books, and following her teachings. My school friends saw the change in me. An old friend recently recalled how I used to chant my mantra during our 45-minute walk together to school and how I would speak only about Amma. She said that she used to admire my focus. That is the transformation Amma can bring into ordinary lives.

When I asked Amma if I could join the ashram, she told me to complete my education. She said that to serve the world, one must be properly equipped. "I can get thousands of people to sweep. The world judges a person with the yardstick of educational qualification. The world does not acknowledge an uneducated person, whereas it will respect people with a postgraduate degree, or a doctor or engineer."

After two years, when I completed my 12th grade, Amma allowed me to join the ashram in 1991, but she told me to enroll for a degree in a local college. I agreed. I just wanted to be with Amma. Going to college was just an excuse to be with Amma in Amritapuri, to do sadhana and seva.

There were different types of sevas—sand seva, cow dung seva, septic tank seva, bathroom cleaning seva, firewood seva, brick seva, kitchen seva, canteen seva, dish washing seva, sweeping seva... We would go to college, study, and do our seva and sadhana. We would stay up at night, participate in ashram activities, and go to college the next day without much sleep.

Once, Amma found many unused objects lying behind the *kalari*.[6] She began to clean up the place. We started helping her. Suddenly, I found myself face to face with Amma, who said, "You people have to become mothers tomorrow..." and Amma began a discourse on *shraddha* (faith and attentiveness) and its importance in spiritual life. I spaced out on hearing 'Become mothers tomorrow.' Was Amma hinting that I would get married and have children? Fear gripped me! Reading my thoughts, Amma said, "When I say mother, I did not mean that you will marry, have children and become a mother. You will become mothers of the world."

I obtained permission from Amma to sit behind her during darshan and study. This way, I could study and, at the same time, be with Amma. Actually, I was not interested in studies at all. The lectures in college were in Malayalam, which I did not understand as I am not a Malayalee; my mother tongue is Tamil. I used to sit in the last row, keep Amma's photo on the desk, chant my mantra, and meditate with eyes open, looking at Amma's photo.

---

[6] Ancestral shrine, where Amma used to give Devi Bhava and Krishna Bhava darshan.

One day, my lecturer stood beside me. I did not even realize his presence. Seeing what I was up to, he yelled at me.

I failed three examinations in the first year of my degree course. It was the first time I had failed in my life. I went to Amma, who was carrying a bag of sand on her back. She asked me, "How did you do in your exams?" I told her that I failed three papers. Amma dropped the bag of sand and glared at me. She said, "The world will blame me for having ruined your future. Have you come here to bring me disgrace and shame? I have lost faith in you." She stopped her seva and went to her room! I was devastated.

Back in Mumbai, I used to do sadhana, attend every program, attend Amma's programs, and still pass all my examinations, by Amma's grace. I was just a devotee then, whereas I was living with her now. I should have passed. I should have received more of her grace.

I did not know it then, but Amma's scolding was a form of divine grace. She began to shoo me away whenever she saw me; it was 'shoo at sight.' I thought Amma hated the sight of me. But after shooing me away, Amma would tell others, "She's very intelligent. She used to get good marks. Now she is not studying. She's following me. That's why I'm being strict with her."

I began to focus on my studies. I led a balanced life of seva, sadhana, *svadhyaya* (scriptural study) and academic studies. I also spent time with Amma. I passed my examinations with decent grades.

Amma once told me, "You will wonder why Amma is being so hard, so strict, why she is scolding you all the time. When you grow up and look back, you will realize why Amma did it and how much she loves you."

Yes, it's true. Back then, I used to feel miserable all the time, thinking that Amma did not love me, how unfortunate I was, etc.

I would be so focused on figuring out how best to win Amma's love.

After I completed my Bachelor of Commerce degree, Amma told me to pursue postgraduate studies. Later, she asked many of the brahmacharinis to pursue the Bachelor of Education (B.Ed.) course. Before our exams, Amma called all of us to her room and gave each one of us a mango from the mango tree adjacent to her room. All of us passed the exams. We call it the *'Manga B.Ed'* meaning 'Mango B.Ed'. Amma gave us the *'jnana pazham'* — the fruit of knowledge. Her prasad is now helping us fulfil her mission of imparting value-based education to society. Most of us are now principals in various Amrita Vidyalayam schools.

Around 1999, I injured my back. For almost a year, I was bedridden. I could not even get up, let alone be with Amma. I stopped singing with Amma and the swamis, touring with Amma, and doing seva. I was unable to sit for even 10 mantras of the *Ashtottharam* (108 attributes of Amma), never mind the *Lalita Sahasranama* (1,000 names of the Divine Mother) during the morning archana. I would lie down in the hall and chant. I began to feel guilty and wondered if my devotion and desire to do sadhana had decreased. I was in physical pain and mentally agonized. When Amma returned from her World Tour, I told Amma tearfully, "Amma, my back is hurting..."

Before I could finish, Amma said aloud, "Your disc has slipped," and told me to consult a doctor in Nairs' Hospital, Kollam. She said I had to undergo traction. When I hesitated, she reprimanded me: "Just do what I say! You don't want to undergo a spinal surgery, do you?"

An MRI revealed that it was a second-grade protrusion. If I was not careful, I would soon have a prolapsed disc. Then, the only option would be surgery, which was highly risky. How did

Amma know all this without even a simple examination or an MRI report? The answer can be found in the *Bhagavad Gita*:

sarvabhutasthamatmanam sarvabhutani catmani
ikshate yogayuktatma sarvatra samadarshanah

The person of spiritual insight, established in same-sightedness, sees the Self as residing in all beings and all beings as resting in the Self. (6.29)

In 2001, Amma sent me to console the victims of the Gujarat earthquake. In the places I visited, I realized that people who lost everything were still positive and clinging to God with faith. Such was their surrender. They had no complaints. I realized that Amma had sent me there not to help them but to learn a big lesson of life. I prayed and I taught the Gujaratis to pray thus: "*Shakti do jagadambe, bhakti do jagadambe, prem do jagadambe, vishwas dekar rakshakaro amriteshwari ma*" — "O Mother of the Universe, give me strength, devotion, love and faith, and thus save me, O Amriteshwari!"

In 2003, I was posted to Mauritius. When Amma told me to go there, I expressed fear and insecurity. Amma said, "Just go. Things will happen. Amma is with you."

Mauritius is beautiful and known as paradise on earth. People are loving. The ashram there is also beautiful. Yet I used to feel homesick, missing Amma and Amritapuri. At night, I would walk about, chanting my mantra and listening to bhajans. At the altar, there was a beautiful photo of Amma smiling. Looking at the photo, I would ask her, "You call yourself a mother? Do you have love or compassion? You have not even bothered to inquire if I am dead or alive, happy or sad!"

One day, as I was looking at the photo and talking to Amma, I felt as if I received an answer from the photo: "I know you are okay. I am with you, protecting you."

I was staying all alone. The temple was on the ground floor. My room was upstairs. Anyone who came to the temple could go upstairs. I felt vulnerable and unsafe. Amma called me, and I told her about how unsafe I felt. She said, "Lock the iron gate at the stairs leading up."

I told her, "There is no gate!"

Amma said, "Look carefully: there's a white iron gate. Keep it locked. No one will be able to go upstairs."

After the conversation with Amma, I looked for the gate. To my surprise, there was an iron gate, painted white to camouflage it with the wall.

One day, a woman devotee took me for a house visit to her friend's house. Her friend, a man, said, "Brahmachariniji, I want to ask you something. You stay alone in that place. What if someone enters the temple while you are doing puja and tries to assault you?"

I was shocked! No one had ever asked me such a question. Praying to Amma, I answered, "My faith is that such a thing will not happen to me."

But the man persisted. "I know that you believe in your Guru and God. Nevertheless, something like that might happen. After all, you are alone there and people know that."

I was annoyed and repeated, "My faith is that such a thing won't happen to me."

But the man kept repeating the same thing and I kept giving him the same answer, more emphatically each time. The devotee who took me to the house scolded the man. We left the house and the devotee apologized profusely for his behavior.

One afternoon, while I was doing the noon puja, four men who looked like thugs came to the temple. They did not look at the deities but at me. I had never seen these men before. Suddenly, I recalled the question I had been asked during the house visit. My mind began oscillating between fear and faith. I prayed fervently to Amma.

Suddenly, from nowhere, a woman appeared. There was a heated conversation between her and the men. The woman became furious and started shouting at the men. I concentrated hard and focused on the puja. After a while, there was pin drop silence. I continued and finished my puja. When I stepped out of the temple, I saw this woman cleaning the temple premises. In broken English, she said, "Those men, bad people! Intention not good! I shouted! I got angry! I sent them away! You don't worry. You are protected."

I asked her where she was from, as I had never seen her before. She said that she lived far away and rarely comes. She went away soon after that. I never saw her again. No prizes for guessing the identity of that mystery woman!

One day, a man asked me to do *Shani* (Saturn) *puja* for him. He asked, "What percentage of Shani do you remove? What are the rates for removing different percentages of Shani?"

I did not know the answer. Yet, by Amma's infinite grace, the knowledge flowed into me and I answered him. I don't remember what I said because the answer did not come from me but from Amma. He left the temple satisfied. I received a good payment, my first earning for Amma. I wanted to share my joy with Amma. To my surprise, she called and asked, "How are you, daughter?"

I excitedly told her about the earnings. Amma laughed. I then asked about the percentage of Shani that would be removed. Amma laughed and said that the percentage depends on his percentage of faith and surrender.

While I was in Mauritius, I developed high blood sugar and cholesterol levels. At that time, I received an email from one of my ashram sisters writing on behalf of Amma: "Dear daughter, how are you? It has been a long time since I heard from you. Amma is worried about you. How is your health? Are you okay? If there is any problem, please tell Amma. Only then can Amma save you."

I replied, "Physically, I'm sick. I have diabetes and cholesterol. Mentally, I'm depressed. Emotionally, I'm broken. I'm fed up! Do not be surprised if I leave this path. I may not be able to hold on."

Amma asked me to return. When I reached Amritapuri, Amma said, "She came back so soon!"

When I replied that I had done so only because Amma told me to, she denied having done so. I said, "I don't think I've done wrong. A fish out of water is desperate to get back into water. A child who is being breastfed, if pulled away, will cling to its mother's bosom."

During a South Indian Tour, I did not get any opportunity to sit near Amma. I was extremely sad and mad at everyone, including myself and even Amma. I decided to discontinue the tour. When I made that decision, we were having a tea stop, near a big field of sugarcane crops that were so much taller than I. I disappeared among the crops. Somehow, a few brahmacharinis learned about my plan. They informed Bri. Bhavamritaji (who was in charge of us), who set out to look for me. She found me and persuaded me to board the bus, promising that she would give me a spot right under Amma's nose at the next stop. Amma's camper was pulling out. She was at the door. As the camper went past me, Amma looked at me with so much pity and love. She told the swamini with her, "She's sad that she did not get me!"

I became depressed. I cursed my birth and life. I wanted to be like those who are always around Amma, interacting with her on the physical level. As soon as we reached Amritapuri, I wrote out all my sorrows to Amma and then went to her room. The door was open. I stood there, the crumpled letter inside my clenched fist, hidden under the loose end of my sari. Amma and I stood facing each other, eye to eye. Amma stretched out her hand. How did she know that I had come with a letter?

Amma said, "You cannot complain that you don't have grace. Do not look at the sun and wish that you could be the sun. Be happy being a firefly. You sing with me. How many people in the ashram get to sing with me? How can you say you don't have grace? There are people in the world who do not have even one person to love them, whereas so many people love you. Whenever Amma looks at anybody, or talks, laughs and jokes with anybody, you should think that Amma is looking at you, laughing and joking with you. You should have the faith that you are Amma's darling child."

I thought, "Yeah, right! Easier said than done. How can I feel happy looking at others having a nice time with Amma?"

After that, whenever I saw Amma talking to someone, as usual, my mind would wonder who the lucky person was. Then, I would recall Amma's advice and tell myself, "Amma is talking to me, laughing with me, joking with me. I am her favorite child."

Initially, I felt cynical about this exercise. But I soon began to realize that my jealousy was diminishing day by day. Eventually, the worms of jealousy stopped gnawing me. I started to enjoy the exercise. I became peaceful. Things changed a lot for me. I began to appreciate life and count my blessings. Amma was opening up the flower of my heart. Had I not received this initiation to practice this kind of visualization, my spiritual life might even have come to an end.

I have been in Gujarat since 2006. Amma made me the principal of the Ahmedabad Amrita Vidyalayam, and Bri. Atmamrita

Chaitanya is the school manager. We both also serve as required in Amma's Gujarat Centre.

I once asked Amma, "What karma have I done to be destined to remain physically separate from you? Am I such a sinner?"

Amma replied, "Daughter, I wouldn't call it sin. What's the benefit of physical closeness when it does not serve its purpose? A ladle in a pot of pudding does not become sweet. Similarly, just being physically close to me will not benefit you. Don't be sad, thinking this way."

The truth is that, wherever we are, we should try our best to transform that place into Amrita's Puri, or Amma's abode.

Once, when I returned to Amritapuri from Gujarat, Amma asked me about the dosage of my thyroid medication. I told her that I was taking 5 mg twice daily. Amma said, "Take 50 mg. Don't stop taking this medicine. You should take it for the rest of your life." Many years before that, while I was still in college, Amma had once told me, out of the blue, "Amma feels you have thyroid. Please go to the Trivandrum Medical College for a thyroid test."

The test proved that I was hyperthyroidic. How had Amma known then? And why was she asking me to increase the dosage now? I called up a doctor, who said that the dosage Amma pre-scribed was for hypothyroidism whereas I have hyperthyroidism. He suggested that I go for a test. To my surprise, the test showed that my hyperthyroidism had changed to hypothyroidism without showing any symptom; the doctor added that this was not a common occurrence. Amma's words over the years have shown me clearly that not only does she know about our thoughts and emotions, she knows each and every molecule in the body. Her vision is holistic and complete.

During a North Indian Tour, Amma went swimming in River Narmada. The waters were shallow. The entire group followed her, not realizing that there was a big dip in the river bed. Suddenly, everyone started drowning. The first thought that came to mind was, "Amma, you have ditched me! I am far behind You. You will save only those close to you!"

They say that one who is drowning resurfaces twice, before sinking the third time. I, too, surfaced twice. Just before sinking again, I thought to myself, "Death is certain. What will you do? Chant 'Amma... Amma...' Think of Amma as you die."

I did that, and suddenly, I found myself thrown on the shore. I was saved! Everyone was saved, for that matter.

Many years later, during another swimming event, Amma asked aloud, "All those who almost drowned in the Narmada, raise your hands!" I raised mine. Amma asked, "What was going through your minds at that time?" I was among those who answered. Amma looked pleased with my answer.

Having lived with Amma all these years has made me understand that obedience, faith and surrender to Amma are the best protection, no matter how difficult and testing life becomes. Avatars like Amma are omniscient, omnipotent and omnipresent. This is why Amma's children are able to experience her presence within and without. This is also why we experience that she knows our heart and feels our pain. Out of utmost compassion, Amma tries her best to alleviate our miseries, which are caused by ignorance. She showers her unconditional love, and gives us both knowledge and strength to overcome our miseries.

There is nothing we can offer in return to Amma. May we all become fit instruments in her divine hands. ௧௨௨

18

Taking Refuge at Her Feet

Br. *Atmaniratamrita Chaitanya*

There was a pond where a fisherman used to fish. Whenever he came, the fish would panic. A veteran fish, who knew every nook and corner of the pond, would hide and watch sadly as his family and friends were caught. However, there was a small fish who was always happy and fearless. It danced and swam, and never got caught. Seeing the carefree play of this little fish, the veteran fish asked him, "How is it that you're so happy, and manage to evade the fishing net every time?"

The little fish said, "It's very simple, Grandpa. The fisherman announces his intention to catch us by first stepping into the water. As soon as he steps in, the water gets disturbed and murky. All the fish start panicking and dart hither and thither. I stop whatever I'm doing and swim as fast as I can to the fisherman's feet before he casts his net. I remain there, away from the net, until he leaves our pond."

Likewise, if we take refuge at the feet of the Lord, we can also elude the snares of worldly life. What does taking refuge mean? It means having an attitude of devotion and surrender to God. Lord Krishna says,

> *api cet su-duracaro bhajate mam ananya-bhak*
> *sadhur eva sa mantavyah samyag vyavasito hi sah*

> Even if the worst sinners worship me with one-pointed devotion, they are to be considered righteous, for they have resolved properly. (*Bhagavad Gita*, 9.30)

This verse glorifies *bhakti* (devotion). Unlike *jnana yoga* (the path of knowledge), which requires many preparatory disciplines, there are no prerequisites for becoming a *bhakta* (devotee).

The Lord says that there are four kinds of devotees: *artha*—one who prays to God to be saved from distress; *artharthi*—one who worships God for material prosperity and pleasure; *jijnasa*—one who desires to know God; and *jnani*—one who knows God. (*Bhagavad Gita*, 7.16)

A key feature of *bhakti yoga*, the path of devotion, is *kripa*. It can mean grace, mercy or blessing, depending on the context. According to the 6th chapter of the *Bhagavad Gita*, one needs four types of kripa: *atma kripa* (one's own grace) *isvara kripa* (God's grace), *sastra kripa* (grace of the scriptures), and *guru kripa* (grace of the Guru).

Atma kripa helps us overcome guilt and boosts our self-confidence. Guilt arises when we feel we have done wrong, and judge ourselves to be sinners. This can be a big obstacle in spiritual life, preventing us from forgiving ourselves. Confidence, the antidote, is the conviction that "even if I have made mistakes, I can correct myself and grow spiritually." Lord Krishna declares that even the worst sinner can become a devotee. '*Duracara*' refers to evil, immoral, corrupt or illegal conduct. '*Suduracara*' means extremely corrupt, and suggests someone who has committed the worst sins. According to the merciful Lord, even such a person need not worry if he gains *ananya-bhakti* (one-pointed devotion). That person will receive God's grace; so guarantees the Lord. Once grace anoints him,

kshipram bhavati dharmatma shashvacchantim nigacchati
kaunteya pratijanihi na me bhaktah pranashyati

Soon he becomes a noble soul and certainly attains
lasting peace. O Arjuna, declare boldly that no devotee of
mine is ever lost. (*Bhagavad Gita*, 9.31)

Such a devotee, who has resolved rightly, starts to gives more
importance to *dharma* (righteousness) than to *artha* (material
prosperity) or *kama* (desire), which had been of primary consider-
ation to him. With increasing spiritual maturity, material things
become less important. While he still uses material things, he is
not so attached to them. A mature soul is dedicated to the pursuits
of dharma and *moksha* (spiritual liberation).

Lord Krishna says that the devotee soon becomes a jijnasu, one
who longs to know God, because he has realized that God is the
only source of peace, security and happiness. When this longing
is consummated, wisdom dawns and the devotee becomes a jnani,
a knower of the Truth. Such a person is never disturbed by the
vicissitudes of life, is ever peaceful and remains devoted to the
Lord; such a devotee will never come to ruin.

Let me recount how someone, who might well have been
considered a sinner, was transformed upon contact with Amma.
I met Surya during the 1992 Chennai Brahmasthanam Temple
programs. He lived near the ashram, was a regular devotee, and
seemed to come from a cultured family. However, he always
looked sad. One day, he revealed the cause of his sorrow. His
father, who was well employed and earning a handsome salary,
was addicted to alcohol. He would come home drunk every
night, and beat his wife. Surya's mother could never stand up to
his father.

I urged Surya to bring his father to Amma. He tried to persuade his father to see Amma but failed. He persisted for another year, pleading with him to meet her at least once. Finally, the father agreed, provided Surya bought him a bottle of wine. The son agreed.

Surya, his mother, brother and father lined up for darshan. I stood behind the father to ensure that he would not change his mind and slip away. As the queue moved towards Amma, the father would take sips from the bottle, which was tucked into a pocket of his pants.

Finally, the family reached Amma. Unable to control herself, Surya's mother fell weeping into Amma's lap. Her body was covered with bruises from beatings. Amma's eyes welled up with tears. Using her own sari, she wiped away the tears from the woman's cheeks. Surya's brother, who was next in line for darshan, stepped aside and hastily pushed his father toward Amma instead. The father was stunned when he found himself in front of Amma.

Amma looked deeply into the father's eyes. Very sweetly and with utmost love, she said, "*Mone* (son)..."

Surya's father burst into tears and fell into Amma's lap. After some time, she raised him, wiped away his tears, and rubbed his chest. Then, pointing to his family members, who were crying, she said, "Son, the next time you drink, remember that you are drinking their tears." She then consoled him, saying, "Don't worry. Amma is with you."

Darshan ended and I accompanied the family back home. After walking some distance, Surya's father put his hand into his pocket to get the wine bottle. He took it out for a few moments and then put it back without opening it. This happened a couple of times. When they reached home, he took the bottle out from his pocket and hurled it into the gutter. He exclaimed "Where have you led me? That woman's voice is still echoing in my ears, '*Mone... mone... mone...*' I can't drink at all!"

The next day, Surya told me what had happened after they reached home. There had been total silence. His father had sat with his eyes closed throughout the night. Early the next morning, to everyone's surprise, he bathed and got ready to accompany his wife and children to Amma's program.

Surya's father completely gave up drinking, and a noticeable, positive change took place over time. Turning to Amma just once helped him turn over a new leaf. Just one hug, one look and one instruction were powerful enough to transform him. So many people have been changed by just one meeting with Amma.

One brahmachari in the ashram was moved when he heard about the qualities of a true devotee. He also heard a talk given by one of Amma's senior disciples on bhakti yoga, and spent some time reflecting on the 36 qualities of a devotee (mentioned in chapter 12 of the *Bhagavad Gita*). One day, when he came for Amma's darshan, he chanted the relevant verses to her and said, "Amma, I don't have even one of these qualities. Will Amma still love me?"

Amma smiled and said, "More than those who have all these 36 qualities, I like the children who strive to attain these qualities!" Isn't this proof that her grace flows to those who try?

Divine grace is always present. We simply have to open our hearts to receive it. Amma will never forsake anyone who is sincere in their spiritual efforts. May her love and compassion inspire devotion in us, and may our devotion draw her closer to us. ᠗᠗

19

Ma-Om Meditation

Br. Kamaleshwaramrita Chaitanya

The Ma-Om meditation is a unique meditation technique born of Amma's *sankalpa* (divine resolve). It is her gift to her children. 'Ma' represents divine love, and 'Om' represents divine light. For this reason, the Ma-Om meditation is also called the 'love and light' meditation.

During this meditation, we silently intone 'Ma' while inhaling. This means we are taking in divine love and letting it permeate all the cells of the body, as the *prana* (vital energy) pervades the whole body. Likewise, when we exhale, we silently intone 'Om,' and feel divine light illuminating the whole body. Gradually, the vibrations of 'Ma' and 'Om' culminate in silence. This is *prana upasana* (worship of the vital energy), which is none other than worship of God, for prana is nothing other than Brahman, the supreme reality.

Whenever Amma gives a talk, she begins by saying, "Amma bows down to all, who are the embodiments of supreme love (*prema-svarup*) and divine consciousness (*atma-svarup*)." By doing so, she reminds us that we are not just body and mind but embodiments of love (Ma) and the all-pervading Self (Om).

Om represents '*nirguna Brahman*' (unmanifested supreme consciousness). Ma represents '*saguna Brahman*' (the manifest form of consciousness, i.e. the world and all its beings and objects).

Sri Ramakrishna Paramahamsa, the renowned 19th-century mystic and saint from Bengal, used to say, "My mother Kali is

Brahman. When she exists alone in her unmanifested state, she's called Brahman, and when she manifests as the world and all its beings, she's called Kali. The world that we see is her *lila* (divine play)."

In the bhajan *'Kali maheshvariye...'* Amma sings, *"Valum talayumilla prapancattin veru ni ennu kelppu"* — "They say that you are the root of the universe, one that has neither head nor tail." These words hint at how the world of names and forms is but a manifestation of the infinite (i.e. without beginning or ending).

It is difficult to worship or focus on nirguna Brahman whereas it is comparatively easier to worship saguna Brahman, because the human intellect can grasp forms more easily than the formless.

'Ma' denotes *'prakriti'* (matter) whereas 'Om' denotes *'purusha'* (consciousness). Prakriti is the feminine aspect of existence, and often personified as Shakti — cosmic will and energy. The counterpoint is the principle of stillness, personified by Shiva, the masculine principle. The image of Kali standing on Shiva's chest illustrates that all movement is founded on a substratum of stillness.

Amma represents both Shiva and Shakti, as all her activities are rooted in perfect stillness. We thus worship her with the mantra *'Om shiva-shakti-aikya rupinyai namah'* — 'Salutations to the Divine Mother, who is the union of Shiva and Shakti in one form' (*Lalita Sahasranama*, 999).

'Ma' and 'Om' are like Amma's eyes in the same way that the moon and sun are poetically considered the eyes of God. In her, we see the perfect blend of divine love and light. She embodies the unconditional love associated with God, and the immeasurable light of her knowledge dispels the darkness of ignorance. Her love is like the coolness of the moon that soothes hearts, whereas her light is like the sun that drives away the night of ignorance.

In the bhajan *'Jnanakkadal,'* the poet says that a small fish cannot measure the depth of the ocean:

jnanakkadal tannai meen alakkalama? Alakkindrapotu sirikkindray taye.

Can a fish measure the depth of the ocean of knowledge? When it attempts to do so, you laugh, O Mother!

Similarly, one cannot measure the vastness and depths of Amma's knowledge, which is oceanic. In fact, it is more than oceanic. It is as vast as the universe, which we cannot measure. Scientists say that the universe keeps expanding.

One brahmachari said, "'Ma' stands for Amma's mother *bhava* (divine mood) and 'Om' represents her Guru bhava." As a mother, Amma binds us with love. As a Guru, she disciplines us and sheds light on the path to knowledge.

Om
Let us consider the scriptural teachings on Om. The very first verse of the *Mandukya Upanishad* defines Om thus:

idam sarvam iti etat aksharam upavyakshanam bhutam bhavat bhavishyat iti sarvam omkarah eva anyat ca yat trikalatitam tat api omkarah eva

Om is this imperishable word. It is the universe, and this is the exposition of Om. The past, present and future — all that was, is and will be — is Om. All else that may exist beyond the boundaries of time is also Om.

This means that Om signifies Brahman which is beyond time. Ma signifies manifestation, which occurs in the three time periods.

'Ma' and 'Om' are two sides of the same coin. Om alludes to the Creator and Ma alludes to creation. Amma often says that creation and Creator are not two entities but one and the same. The Creator has become creation. She sings, *"Srishtiyum niye, srashtavum niye"*—"You are creation. Creator, too, you are." Amma says her children are not different from her.

Once a journalist asked Amma, "You have so many followers. Do they worship you?"

Amma replied, "I don't know about that. But I worship them." For Amma, her children are her God.

In the *Bhagavad Gita*, Lord Krishna says that he is the *pranava mantra* (Om) in the Vedas (7.8). He further says,

> *om ity ekaksharam brahma vyaharan mam anusmaran*
> *yah prayati tyajan deham sa yati paramam gatim*

One who leaves the body while remembering me (the Supreme) and uttering the monosyllabic Om attains the highest goal. (8.13)

Love (Ma)

Love gives strength, power and wisdom. In the *Tirumandiram*, Lord Tirumular says

> *anbum sivamum irandu enbar arivilaar*
> *anbe sivamavatu yarum arikilaar*
> *anbe sivamavatu yarum arintapin*
> *anbe sivamay amarntu iruntare*

The ignorant foolishly say that love and Shiva are two.
None know that Shiva is nothing other than love.
When one realizes that love and Shiva are the same,
One becomes the very embodiment of love. (270)

Here, love represents Ma, and Shiva represents Om. When we
understand that love is not separate from the Lord, we become
embodiments of love. Ma is Om, and Om is Ma. That is why,
during meditation, Amma tells us that we can alternate intoning
Ma and Om with Om and Ma while inhaling and exhaling.

Ma means 'mother' in almost all the cultures of the world. The
mother is synonymous with love, and maternal love is the highest
form of love in mundane life.

The first mantra of the *Lalita Sahasranama* is *'Om shri matre
namah'* — 'Salutations to the auspicious Mother.' This mantra
contains both 'Ma' and 'Om' and points to the fundamental
importance of both in spiritual life.

Amma says that the defining characteristics of motherhood
are forgiving and forbearing, both of which arise from love. She is
the embodiment of divine motherhood. Her love is immeasurable,
and her patience, greater than that of Mother Earth.

Amma does not expect anything from us. She continues her
mission of unconditionally loving, serving and uplifting others.
Amma's love for us helps us assimilate her divine qualities and
nourishes our spiritual growth.

Once, when Amma saw an elderly devotee walking away to
wash his plate after he had finished eating, she told me to wash
his plate. She said, "If he were your father, wouldn't you wash his
plate? Take the plates from elderly devotees and wash the plates!"

Amma also teaches ashram residents to greet devotees with
the words *'Om namah shivaya'* ('Salutations to the auspicious')
and inquire if they have received accommodation and food.

Through such simple instructions, Amma teaches us to love and serve the world without expectation. For Amma, the whole world is her family. She is also trying to elevate us to this level of understanding. This is the light of wisdom, and is poetically said to emanate from the third eye.

There are instances galore that reveal the magnitude of Amma's unconditional love. Years ago, during Amma's Chennai Brahmasthanam temple festival, a leper who had been healed but still bore visible scars, came to see Amma. His family and friends had disowned him, and did not want to have anything to do with him even after he was healed. He led the life of a vagabond, surviving on whatever providence offered him.

When he heard about Amma and her program in Chennai, he wanted to have her darshan. At the Chennai ashram, Amma gazed at him with love and an enigmatic smile. Her look suggested that she knew all about him. Amma did not say anything but continued looking at him, as if waiting for him to speak. With some hesitation, the man disclosed his problems to Amma, who kept nodding her head, encouraging him to speak. Amma then called the swami in charge of the Chennai ashram and asked him how many of the newly-constructed Amrita Kuteerams (houses the ashram builds for the homeless poor) in Chennai were vacant. She then instructed him to give one of the houses to this man. The man was dumbstruck. Amma hugged him warmly and intoned words of love and consolation in his ears. He broke down. He had never received so much love from anyone, including his own mother. How many such lives have been uplifted by Amma's love!

In a sense, we are all afflicted by inner leprosy. We carry wounds caused by angry words, rejection, bitter experiences, and by our own negativities such as lust, anger, jealousy and pride. It must have been infinitely easier for Amma to heal Dattan,[7] the leper, than it is for her to heal our inner wounds. But she is doing so through her divine compassion.

Sometimes, Amma demonstrates 'tough love' — love that wears the mask of sternness. Amma often says that, in this day and age, only *Kamsa-bhakti* can take us closer to God. Kamsa, Lord Krishna's uncle, lived in terror from the day Krishna was born because of the prophecy that his nephew would kill him. Amma was born to slay the Kamsa-ego in all of us, and it is the ego that instinctively fears Amma.

Amma wields the sword of knowledge to remove our ignorance. But we need not fear, for Amma will administer the anesthesia of divine love. If we stop resisting, she can remove our ego and kindle the light of knowledge in us.

Everyone is conditioned by likes and dislikes. This conditioning makes it difficult for us to love others unconditionally, the way Amma does. She is helping us rise above our likes and dislikes, and to do so, she might have to wear the mask of Kali occasionally. But let us never forget that behind the fearsome mask is a heart overflowing with unfathomable love.

Whatever Amma does is for our spiritual growth. The Guru's aim is to help the disciple attain Self-realization. No matter what our state of spiritual understanding, Amma meets us at that level.

Sometimes, during darshan, Amma tells devotees, "Your shirt (or sari) is really nice!" Hearing this, the devotee feels overjoyed. He or she may not remember Amma's satsang, but will remember this one remark. In this way, Amma helps the devotee forge a connection with her.

To a scientist, Amma might discuss his area of research. To one involved in cyber security, she might speak about the different

---

[7] A reference to a leper who used to visit Amma in Amritapuri; Amma would lick and suck the pus out from his wounds, and thus healed him.

levels of security measures that need to be implemented. To a person working in the field of wireless networks, she might point out where wireless sensors are to be deployed. To an Ayurveda doctor, Amma might share her knowledge of various medicinal plants. To simple village women, she might lovingly ask if their husbands still drink, how they are managing the family, and even offer them saris.

After forging a bond of love with us, Amma slowly raises us towards the level of supreme knowledge. She melts our minds with the warmth of love before molding us with the discipline of knowledge.

Amma's love can elevate one from *kamya bhakti* (devotion with selfish motives) to *tattva bhakti* (devotion based on an understanding of spiritual principles) and *nishkama bhakti* (selfless devotion). A man from Tamil Nadu came to see Amma in order to sell his hospital to her. She declined, but by her grace, he was able to sell it later. He became a staunch devotee, and played a vital role in conducting Amma's public programs in Erode, Salem and Vellore. Although he was in his 70s, he worked hard, visiting more than 200 villages in Thiruvannamalai to spread Amma's message and to invite the villagers to attend Amma's program.

He once told Amma, "I can't meditate. But I love serving you by taking your message to villagers in Tamil Nadu."

Amma replied, "Son, that *seva* (selfless service) itself is meditation."

Doing seva with the right attitude is meditation. Such selfless work leads to *citta shuddhi* (purity of mind), which paves the way for *jnana prapti* (attainment of knowledge).

Amma's love is transformative. There was a thug who changed his ways completely after meeting Amma. People who knew him were wonderstruck at the change. When they learnt that he had changed after meeting Amma, they also wanted to meet her. He brought them to Amritapuri during Amma's birthday celebration. His family, friends and relatives are all Amma's devotees now. He gives Amma's photo to anyone he meets.

Where there is true love, there is silence. Love abides in the heart. That love cannot be put into words. A true lover only meditates; he never thinks. When there is only one thought about the beloved, there is no mind. Two become one.

In true love, meditation happens spontaneously. We become silent and remain at rest in our Self. There are no words. That is why Dakshinamurti, regarded as the first Guru, communed in silence.

Goddess Parvati once asked Lord Shiva to teach her how to be one with him always. He asked her to meditate and asked her what she saw. She said that she saw his form. He told her to transcend it. She saw a brilliant light. After transcending it, she heard Om. After she had transcended this sound, she remained silent. She had merged with the Lord and lost her individuality. She attained the final state of love: eternal and inseparable union with God.

Once a man prayed to God: "Please open my heart and fill it with your grace!" He prayed and prayed. God appeared before him and said, "Son, I'm happy that you want to open your heart, but I can't open it because it's closed from the inside. You must open it. I'm waiting to enter and fill it with love and light."

May we all open our hearts to Amma's divine love. May we have an attitude of acceptance and equanimity in all situations. May we become perfect instruments in Amma's hands. May Amma's love and light take us to the supreme knowledge. ৬৯৯৵

20

Awakening
Br. Sundareshamrita Chaitanya

Many of us would have heard the ashram bhajans '*Jago Ma Kali Jago Jago*' and '*Unarunaru Amritanandamayi Unaru Jaganmate.*' The name of the first bhajan means 'Wake up, Mother Kali, wake up!" and that of the second means "Awaken, Mother Amritanandamayi, awaken!"

When I first heard these songs, I wondered why we had to wake Mother Kali or Amma up. Actually, these bhajans are reminding us to awaken the Divine Mother within us. They are calls to awaken our inner divinity. We may consider ourselves wide awake, alert and fully conscious of all that is happening. However, from the perspective of a Self-realized soul and the scriptures, we have been fast asleep throughout life. The only awakened souls are *mahatmas* (spiritually illumined souls) like Amma. For them, the world that we so intensely perceive as real is like a dream. They also see and experience what we do, but they are firmly rooted in their true self. This contrasting difference in the perceptions of ordinary people and Self-realized beings is what Lord Krishna metaphorically expresses in the *Bhagavad Gita*:

> *ya nisha sarvabhutanam tasyam jagarti sanyami*
> *yasyam jagrati bhutani sa nisha pashyato muneh*

Whatever is night to ordinary people is like day for one who has realized the Self. And whatever is day to all beings in the world is night to the introspective sage. (2.69)

This celebrated verse hints at the contrast between the *advaitic* (non-dual) state of a *jnani* (knower of the Truth) and the *dvaitic* (dual) state of an *ajnani* (ignorant one). In the first line, 'night' refers to ignorance regarding Self-knowledge. Just as we can't perceive objects at night, we don't perceive our real nature clearly. Most of us perceive ourselves and other things or beings in this world as independent entities, separate from each other and the world. We see everything in terms of 'me' and 'not me.' This perception of duality is as real as daylight for us.

A transparent crystal on a red cloth appears red because of the proximity between the two. Similarly, we have mistakenly assumed ourselves to be the body, mind and intellect. This mistaken perception has become a strong conditioning for us. In this way, we identify with negative emotions such as fear, anger and greed, and feel that the happiness we gain from sense pleasures is real. We develop attachment towards people, objects and ideologies, which consequently turn into likes and dislikes. In trying to gain what we like and avoid what we dislike, we eventually become trapped in a never-ending cycle of joyful and sorrowful experiences.

However, a jnani perceives his Self in all of creation. Amma often says, "The Creator and creation are not two," and that the Creator has actually become the creation. God pervades the whole of creation as pure awareness, consciousness and love.

Even though a goldsmith makes many varieties of ornaments such as bangles, necklaces, bracelets and rings, he is fully aware that all of them are made of gold, and are thus essentially the same. Similarly, jnanis see the world of plurality, just like us, but at the same time they clearly perceive the unity behind the diversity in creation. Therefore, jnanis do not depend on external objects, people or experiences for their happiness. They are even-minded in all circumstances, and have perfect control over their senses. Amma says, "The happiness that we get from the pleasures of this world is but a minute reflection of the infinite bliss that comes from your own Self."

To indicate a jnani, Lord Krishna uses the word *'samyami,'* which means a person who has complete control over his mind and senses, i.e. has both *shama* and *dama*. Shama is the calmness of mind that arises when *vasanas* (latent tendencies) have been eradicated. A person with shama doesn't give in to desires and is even-minded in all circumstances. Dama refers to the restraint of one's *indriyas* (senses). A samyami keeps his mind united with the intellect and does not allow it to join the indriyas and stray towards sensual objects.

Patanjali's *Yoga Sutras* mention the *Ashtanga Yoga*, or eight 'limbs' (steps) needed to achieve union with the divine. The last three steps are *dharana, dhyana* and *samadhi*. In dharana, one tries to focus his mind on an object or the Self within. In dhyana, the person has attained one-pointed concentration on the object of meditation. In samadhi, the meditator and the object of meditation become one. These three steps are collectively called *'samyama'* and a yogi who practices this and is adept at it is also called a samyami.

Shankaracharya says that a samyami doesn't have *kartrtva bodha*, the egoistic sense that he is a doer. Therefore, the outcome of his actions does not bind him. He performs all actions as an instrument in the hands of God and is able to accept all results as divine will.

———

I first met Amma in June 1996 in Dallas, USA, while pursuing my higher studies. During my very first darshan, Amma hugged me and smilingly asked me in Tamil, *"Amma vantaala?"* ("Has Amma come into your life?")

I smiled and nodded my head but I had no idea what she meant. Amma's darshan and the bhajans that evening made a deep impression on me. I was touched by her unassuming simplicity and humility. I left after the evening bhajans, but my life would not be the same again.

I went to the library in the University of Texas at Austin, where I was a student, and found a copy of Amma's biography. Reading it, I felt deeply moved by her life and resolved to follow her teachings in my life as best as I could. I started attending the weekly bhajans held in a devotee's place in Austin, learnt to chant the *Lalita Sahasranama*, and started reading Amma's *'Awaken, Children'* series. My old friends and old ways of life slowly dropped away, and I found my life heading in a different direction altogether.

The next year, I got a summer internship in Sunnyvale, California, close to Amma's San Ramon Ashram. In those days, Amma used to spend more than two weeks in San Ramon, and I would go every evening and weekend to meet her. During Amma's US tour, I made it a point to go to some of the cities she was visiting, to attend her programs. When I returned to Texas, the responsibility of organizing and conducting Amma's weekly bhajans in Austin fell on my shoulders. Slowly, I began to understand what Amma meant when she said, "Amma vantaala?" She was simply taking over my life! My PhD, which was supposed to be a full-time pursuit, slowly became a 'spare-time' activity.

The desire to join Amma's ashram soon became strong. I began gently hinting to Amma about this and once asked her to find me "a small place in your big organization." She laughed and told me that ashram life was not easy. But I sensed that Amma would agree if I persisted in asking her. Alas, I lacked the courage, as I did not know if I could withstand the rigors of monastic life. I was also worried about how my parents would react. As directed by Amma, I completed my PhD. Even then, I did not have the courage to ask her.

Once, while standing next to Amma as she was giving darshan at night in San Ramon, she sarcastically said, "If you have fear, then go and stand outside in the dark!"

I did not understand the significance of that remark until much later. An avatar like Amma is like the brilliant sun that dispels the darkness of our ignorance. In the *Lalita Sahasranama*, Devi is described as '*ajnana dvanta dipika*'—the bright lamp that dispels the darkness of ignorance. Devi is also described as '*bhakta harda tamo bheda bhanumad bhanu santatih*'—the sunrays that dispel the darkness from devotees' hearts. Living in the presence of a Master like Amma, who is a beacon to millions, is like walking in broad daylight. There is greater clarity in both mundane matters and the spiritual life. In contrast, living in the selfish and material world is like moving about in darkness. Amma was saying that if I had no courage, I would remain in the dark.

About two years after completing my PhD, Amma finally brought me to Amritapuri. I am reminded of lines from a bhajan:

> *amma ki chaya me mera safar*
> *ye teri krpa hai meri ma…*

The journey of life takes place in mother's protective and cool shade. This is solely because of my mother's grace.

> *duniya ki maya sagar mein*
> *dub raha tha meri ma*

balo se pakad ke mujhe
kaise bacaya jagadamba

I was drowning in the illusory ocean of this world. O
Mother, grabbing me by the hair, how did you manage to
save me, O mother?

Arjuna asks Lord Krishna to describe the signs of a jnani — how
he sits, walks, talks, etc. The question was clearly focused on the
outer or gross differences between a jnani and an ajnani. The
Lord's answers allude to the inner or subtle differences pertaining
to one's mental state. From Arjuna's question and Krishna's
answer, we can see that the difference between an ajnani and a
jnani is like night and day.

The gist of this idea is beautifully illustrated in the *Tirumandiram* by Saint Tirumular:

> *marattai maraittatu mamata yanai*
> *marattil maraindatu mamata yanai*
> *parattai maraittana parmudal bhutam*
> *parattil maraindana parmudal bhutame*

The wood is concealed by the figure of the elephant.
The elephant disappears into the wood.
The five gross elements conceal the supreme.
The five gross elements disappear into the supreme.

A child visiting a temple with his father sees a huge figure of an
elephant and becomes frightened. The child's father, a carpenter,
allays his fear, saying that the elephant is not real but wooden,
carved and painted so well that it looks real. To the child, the

elephant was real, whereas to the carpenter, the wood was real. Similarly, for ordinary people who perceive the material world constituted of the five gross elements, the supreme principle is hidden. But a jnani sees the supreme principle clearly, and the material world is as if non-existent for him.

Amma conveys the same message through this vivid analogy: "During the arati in temples, all other lights are either dimmed or turned off, and only the light of the oil lamp or camphor being waved in front of the idol remains. This represents the principle that it is only when we turn away from external sense objects that we discover the light within."

Consider a boat. If the weather is calm, it moves steadily. However, in rough weather, the boat can be tossed about easily. But a submarine will hardly be affected even if there is a thunderstorm or severe winds. We are like a boat, easily affected by turbulent circumstances affecting body or mind. But a samyami is like the submarine, unaffected by outer circumstances. If we can dive deep within ourselves, we will attain a tranquil mind.

Amma says, "When the waves of our turbulent mind subside, the motionless substratum shines forth. That substratum is the essence of religion. God is present in each one of us, in all beings and things." But because of our attachment to people and objects, we do not perceive the underlying essence. If we practice even a little detachment, Amma will reward us generously.

I am reminded of an incident that happened while I was still studying in the US. My Mexican roommate, who used to practice Chinese medicine and acupuncture, was also a devotee of Amma. When he was going to return permanently to Mexico, I decided to give him a small gift as a token of our friendship. At that time, I had a beautiful photo of Amma's feet. It was a rare photo that I had bought recently. I was strongly attached to it and used to worship it daily. Amma teaches that one way to develop detachment towards material objects is to give away objects to which we are strongly attached. I decided to give my friend this photo as a parting gift in an attempt to develop detachment. He accepted the gift happily.

After he left, I began missing the photo badly. I asked myself, "Why did I give away that photo? I could've given him something else instead!"

Shortly thereafter, just before Amma arrived in Dallas, I received a call from the organizers of the Dallas program, asking me if I wanted to do *pada puja* to Amma as she entered the darshan hall. This was surprising because, in those days, they usually gave such opportunities only to devotees who had been seeing Amma for many years; at that point, I had known Amma for less than two years. Doing pada puja to Amma was a dream come true for me, and I immediately accepted the invitation. By giving up the cherished photo of her feet, I was blessed with the opportunity to perform pada puja to her real feet. I took this as a message from Amma that if I can give up my attachments to material objects, then the rewards will bring me greater joy. (I'm not saying we should not be attached to photos of Amma.)

Ordinary people are unaware of reality in all the three states of consciousness — the waking, deep sleep and dream states. But a jnani, who has awakened to reality, remains a witness in all the three states. Years ago, a group of us used to go to the Madurai Ashram every weekend to conduct satsang-and-bhajan programs. A devotee who was blind from birth used to play the *tabla* for us. Once, we asked him if he had dreams at night and what he saw in his dreams. He said that his dreams were "audio only, no video." So, just as our dream state is an extension of our waking state, our ignorance of our true nature continues in all the three states. Naturally, we do not understand the subtle aspects of the mind and heart even when we are wide awake.

When I was Head of Electronics at Amrita University, I had a student who failed all his subjects in the first year of his Bachelor of Technology (B.Tech.) degree program. According to the rules of the university, he had to repeat the entire first year. Even then, he ended up failing all his exams again. This meant repeating the first year a third time. After discussing the matter with other faculty, I called the boy's parents and advised them that it would be best for the student to pursue a non-engineering degree as he was not making any progress at all. I also explained that he would not only end up paying more in college fees, but would also end up losing a few years from his career.

The student was unhappy but did not say anything. I took him and his father to meet Amma and told her what we had decided. Amma smiled at the boy compassionately and asked him "Son, do you want to leave? Don't you want an engineering degree?"

With tears in his eyes, the student said that he knew he had not been applying himself to his studies, but wanted another chance. With Amma's approval, he continued to study there and began performing better. Later, I learnt that during his holidays, he used to participate in ashram activities and had become attached to Amma and the ashram. Therefore, he did not want to leave this hallowed atmosphere. Amma was able to clearly see his heart whereas we could not. Eventually, by Amma's grace, he completed his degree and now has a good job in Bangalore.

What looks like unintelligible scribbles to the uninitiated might actually be a masterpiece—a priceless depiction of human emotions and human psyche—in the eyes of a connoisseur. Similarly, we may not be able to make much sense of the seemingly chaotic and irrational universe. However, to a jnani, the whole creation is a divine playground. Sri Ramakrishna Paramahamsa said, "This world is a mansion of mirth."

For the Self-realized, there is no fear, sorrow or other negative emotion, only bliss. Although we see the same world as Amma, our experiences are poles apart. Amma has said, "The whole universe is like a bubble inside me." We cannot even try to imagine that state. We may see her behaving like one of us, laughing or crying with us. But we should never forget that she is on a completely different plane altogether. Amma is the perfect samyami. She is not at all identified with her body; if she were, she would not have been able to give darshan for so many hours a day for the last 45 years. She eats very little, hardly sleeps, and is able to rise above physical pain and discomfort. No ordinary person can do what Amma has been doing. She is never perturbed by anything, whether a tsunami, a pandemic or problems at her institutions. Amma remains equipoised at all times and focuses on the positive actions she can do.

In order to see the bottom of a lake covered by leaves and scum, we must first remove the dirt, and then wait for the ripples on the lake's surface to subside. Our mind is like a dirty lake. Amma says that we must perform selfless actions with sraddha and compassion, and cultivate an attitude of acceptance. Doing so purifies our mind. Doing spiritual practices like *japa* (repeated chanting of a mantra) and meditation helps to restrain the mind and senses. Then if we look within, by Amma's grace, we can realize our own true nature. Amma says that God's grace is what crowns any endeavor with success. Sri Ramana Maharshi says that the "Guru's grace is the primary and most essential factor for realizing the Self. All other factors are only secondary."

May Amma shower her infinite grace on us all so that we can realize our true nature. ☺☙☙

21

Perfection in Action
Swamini Chitprabhamrita Prana

Years ago, the area where the hall is today was marshy ground. Every day except on the bhava darshan days, there would be sand seva here after dinner. At one end of this plot, there used to be a heap of sand. The satsangs would be held here just before the sand seva.

One day, it was my turn to give a talk. Swami Amritageetananda had assigned me the topic: Bhakti Yoga, on the basis of *Upadesha Saram.*[8] I had joined the ashram not long before this, and as I was unfamiliar with that text, I did not refer to it at all while preparing for the talk. I referred only to what Amma had taught us about Bhakti Yoga. On the morning of the talk, Swami Amritageetananda called me and told me to include specific points from his classes on *Upadesa Saram.* I became nervous, as I had not included any of those points; there was no time either to add any.

That evening after bhajans, just before my satsang was about to begin, I saw Amma sitting alone beside the heap of sand. I went to her, prostrated, and confided my fears in her. "Amma, I

---

[8] Bhakti yoga refers to the path of bhakti (devotion) as a means of attaining union with God. Analogous paths include karma yoga (path of action) and jnana yoga (path of knowledge). Upadesha Saram, literally 'Essence of Spiritual Instruction,' is a work by Sri Ramana Maharshi, a sage from Tiruvannamalai (1879 – 1950).

don't think what I prepared is what Amritageetananda Swami expects. I'm scared! Please be with me."

Amma replied, "Daughter, deliver your satsang fearlessly. Amma will be with you!"

In my anxiety, I hardly heard what Amma was saying. In desperation, I grabbed her hand and said again, "Amma, please be with me!"

Even though only a few people had assembled to hear my talk, I was trembling. As I stood and chanted the *dhyana shloka* (benedictory verse), it started raining. Most of the people gathered there moved to the nearby huts, leaving no one in front of me. I could not leave as I was the speaker. I noticed someone walking towards me with a big, white umbrella. As I was engrossed in the satsang, I did not look to see who it was. The person carrying the umbrella reached me and whispered into my ears, "*Mookke* (nickname Amma gave me, referring to my prominent nose), speak boldly!"

It was Amma herself, standing right next to me, holding the umbrella to shield me from the rain! I was wonderstruck and touched that Amma had fulfilled her promise ("Amma will be with you!") literally.

I first met Amma in 1985 when I was in ninth grade. My father had gone to see Amma first. She asked him, "Why didn't you bring your children?"

So, he took our whole family to meet Amma. My family revered and frequently visited *mahatmas* (spiritually illumined souls). Initially, I was hesitant about meeting Amma, as we had made other plans for the day. My idea of a mahatma, based on those I had met over the years, was that of an old man with matted locks and a flowing white beard. When my father said, "Amma is a beautiful 32-year-old *yogini* with deep, black shining eyes, a sparkling nose-ring and a captivating smile," I agreed to visit

Amma. We went to see her in the evening. Before seeing Amma, I heard her voice. She was singing bhajans. Hearing that voice, I felt as if I had been transported to a totally different realm. Her voice seemed out of this world. When I saw Amma and her children sing, I even wondered if they were really of this world. The atmosphere was charged with divinity. I was so entranced that I did not realize that the bhajans ended and Amma was giving darshan. There were very few people present. Back then, Amma used to give out sacred ash directly (not in packets). She gave some to me, applied some on my forehead, and kissed me. With a mischievous smile, Amma said, "O daughter, you have come! Keep coming!"

After my family members and I had our darshan, I realized that Amma had smeared sacred ash only on my forehead and not on those of my family members. I felt that I belonged to Amma. "That's why she gave me this special treatment!" I thought egotistically.

After this meeting, my thoughts were irresistibly drawn towards Amma. I was longing to be with her again. This was my first experience of overflowing love.

I enrolled in a college near a devotee's house in Calicut. Whenever Amma visited their home, I would somehow hear about it and go there without my family's knowledge. I would watch Amma practicing bhajans with the brahmacharis.

I used to cry and plead with Amma to let me stay in the ashram. But in those days, girls could only stay in the ashram with their families. Because of this, I did not have much hope of ever being able to stay in the ashram. Over time, Amma started allowing girls to stay as brahmacharinis. She also allowed me to join the ashram. But as I was only in my second year of college then, my father came and took me back home forcibly. I was heartbroken. Later, after I completed my college education, with much difficulty and by Amma's grace alone, I was able to fulfill my long-standing dream of staying permanently with Amma.

Over the years, Amma has blessed me with innumerable experiences that are beautiful and spiritually elevating. Let me share one such precious gem.

After I joined the ashram, I was assigned the seva of doing laundry for the ashram's Western residents who needed help with washing their clothes because of a water shortage in the ashram. At that time, as water was available only on certain days of the week, on the days when there was no water, we (the brahmacharinis assigned this seva) would go across the backwaters to the house of Sajini-chechi (Amma's youngest sister). Initially, a senior brahmacharini taught us how to wash clothes, as we had never washed even our own clothes before joining the ashram. Though there were many clothes to wash, we enjoyed it as Amma would frequently inquire about us. Also, the thought that Amma had touched these clothes during darshan would motivate us to do the seva. One day, Bri. Bindu and I were washing clothes together. One of the items that needed to be washed was a brand-new pair of blue jeans, which was stained here and there. We had been taught to apply a paste of raw bleaching powder to remove stains. Out of ignorance, we applied bleaching powder on all the stains. You can imagine what happened! After we finished washing it, we found big white circles where the stains had been! We had not expected this.

Suddenly, I had a brainwave. I told Bindu, "In the *Bhagavad Gita*, Lord Krishna says, *'Yogah karmasu kaushalam'* ('Yoga is skill in action') (2.50)." At that time, I had misunderstood 'kaushalam' to mean 'cunning' and hence thought that what the Lord meant was, "Get the work done by hook or crook!" I said, "Let's use our kaushalam (cunning). If we apply bleach all over the jeans, we can make the white color uniform." We proceeded to do just that!

The next day, the owner of the jeans complained that they were missing. We told him that we had washed and sent them back, and asked him to check again. After doing so, he came back and said that there was only an old pair; his brand-new blue jeans were missing. We cheekily told him to check the old pair to see if his name was there. On checking, the poor man was shocked to see his name on it. He realized that his new pair of jeans had been reduced to this pitiable condition. Upset, he complained to a senior brahmacharini. When she questioned us, we confessed what we had done. She scolded us severely. Then, to our shock, she told Amma what we had done. Amma summoned and scolded us. She then apologized to the man on our behalf. She told him, "These children are not used to doing such work. They never did so at home, and acted out of ignorance."

Hearing Amma's words, the man calmed down and meekly left without another word.

Turning to us, Amma said, "Children, you should strive to discharge your duties perfectly. When you wash each item of clothing, imagine that you are removing the impurities from your own mind. Every time you remove a stain, imagine that you are removing the impurities accumulated over lifetimes. At the end of each day, visualize yourself offering your cleaned mind to God. When you act in this way, your seva will help to purify your mind. Only then will it become karma yoga."

After this incident, our attitude towards seva changed totally. We used to do the work with a playful attitude. From then on, we started working with utmost attention. We carefully looked for and washed every minute stain in the clothes, looking upon the dirt as reflections of our own mental impurities. In this way, we tried to bring perfection to our actions. Thus, in her own simple way, Amma taught us how to transform *karma* (actions) into karma yoga.

Lord Krishna says,

buddhiyukto jahatiha ubhe sukrita dushkrite
tasmad yogaya yujyasva yogah karmasu kaushalam

Endowed with the wisdom of even-mindedness, one abandons both good and evil deeds. Therefore, dedicate yourself to yoga. Yoga is skill in action. (*Bhagavad Gita*, 2.50)

Roasted seeds will never sprout, even in favorable circumstances. Likewise, the ego of one who has surrendered all actions to God will not rear its head. Lord Krishna advises us never to forget, even while actively engaged in action, that we are neither doers of the deed nor enjoyers of the fruits of action, but mere instruments in the hands of the divine.

We should become totally immersed in what we do but remain unattached at the same time. The nature of action is to bind. Acting in such a way that actions do not bind us is true skill. To illustrate, if we apply oil on our hands before cutting the sticky jackfruit, it will not stick to our hands.

A karma yogi is focused only on gaining mental purity. He is not concerned with the *punya* (merit) or *papa* (demerit) of his actions. It is the law of nature that we will reap what we sow, whether or not we like it. Good deeds produce good results, and bad deeds bring bad results. Acting with discernment and without expecting the fruits of action, thus going beyond punya and papa, is *karma kushalata* (skillful action).

Once, a man named Komu died and his soul ascended heavenwards. He missed his wife and children, and felt lonely and sad. Suddenly, he heard a sweet voice from behind: "Please stop!"

He turned around and beheld a beautiful form. He asked, "Who are you?"

The form said, "I am the result of your good deeds in life. I am coming with you."

Hearing this, the man became happy and resumed his journey, accompanied by his merits. Suddenly, he heard a dreadful voice roaring, "Stop right there!"

When he turned around, he saw a terrifying figure looming large. Trembling in fear, he asked, "Who are you?"

The figure said, "I am the result of the bad deeds you committed. I am also coming with you."

The man said, "I don't want you. I have the pleasant company of my merits with me."

The figure said, "You don't have a choice. I am your own creation and will follow you like a shadow. You should have thought about this before doing the bad deeds in the first place."

That is why the Lord says that we should strive to transcend both merits and demerits. Both are binding. Whereas bad deeds are like an iron chain, good deeds are like a golden chain. That is the only difference.

Amma always tells us to live in the present. When we are wholly immersed in the present moment, there will be awareness and alertness. Such actions become perfect, enjoyable and beautiful. In truth, life is nothing but a continuous succession of present moments.

There are three meanings associated with the word 'present.' It can mean a gift. It can also refer to this moment. It is also associated with presence. Each 'present moment' is a 'present' from God. When our presence is wholly invested in the moment, we can return it to God as an offering or present from us. In other words, actions done with a total surrender of body, mind and intellect become worthy of being offered to God.

Look at Amma. Every action of hers is filled with grace and beauty. She surrenders herself completely to whatever she does. Every one of the thousands of people who come for her darshan gets only a few precious moments with her, but those moments become cherished memories. Those precious moments infuse them with the mental strength and energy to face life's challenges. This is because Amma acts from the realm of the Self, where there is only bliss. A spark of this bliss touches the Self of the person having darshan and inspires him or her to return for darshan. But in order to gain the full benefit of her grace, our mind must be open.

Whenever we are entrusted with a task, we are likely to focus on its most difficult parts. We thus become overwhelmed. This makes the challenge seem so large that our mind loses confidence. We may even give up.

A story comes to mind. A man approached the Buddha and confided that his mind was very disturbed. The Buddha told him to bring some salt, dissolve it in a glass of water, and drink it. It was so salty that the man could not sip more than a drop. The Buddha then told him to bring the same quantity of salt, drop it into a freshwater lake, and to drink the water from the lake. The man could easily drink it, for there was no trace of salt in the lake water. The Buddha said, "In both cases, you added the same amount of salt. The only difference was the amount of water into which you added it. Likewise, everyone encounters problems in life. They are perceived as large or small, depending on the expansiveness of the mind dealing with them."

Amma's life has always been filled with problems and challenges, right from her early days. But no problem creates even the smallest ripple in her vast, universal mind. If an elephant enters a clear pond, the water will become turbid. But if it wades into an ocean, it will make no difference to the ocean. Amma's mind is as deep and all-encompassing as the ocean. In fact, problems will crumble when they encounter Amma's cosmic mind.

We feel disturbed when we encounter problems because our minds are closed and petty. The root cause of such a mind is the ego. Amma uses different tools to eradicate the ego of the disciples. She nurtures values in them and inspires them to act in a way that benefits others. This is the greatest miracle that Amma performs. By her grace, many lives have been transformed.

Every breath of Amma is for the happiness of her children. The physical strain that Amma endures for us is unfathomable.

I remember a story. Once, a little girl sitting in her father's lap asked, "Daddy, mummy's face is so beautiful. But why are her hands black and deformed?"

The father replied, "When you were a baby, the cradle you were sleeping in caught fire. When your mother realized that there was no other way to save you, she took you out from the cradle with her bare hands. The burns she sustained disfigured her hands permanently."

When she heard this, the girl felt that her mother's hands were the most beautiful in the whole world.

Once, a devotee asked Amma why there was a swelling on her left cheek. Amma answered, "It's not that my left cheek is swollen, but my right cheek has become flattened by the constant pressure of holding devotees during darshan."

We can see a dark round mark on her right cheek. Not that Amma has ever complained. In fact, when a devotee asked her about this mark, Amma casually said, "It's the mark of my children's love!"

In China, there is a kind of bamboo tree known as the Chinese Bamboo. The farmer sows the seeds of this tree, adds fertilizer, and waits patiently. In the first year, nothing sprouts. Nevertheless, the farmer continues fertilizing and watering. He does so for three or four years. Finally, in the fifth year, the seed sprouts. The plant starts growing rapidly and reaches a height of 90 – 120 feet within six weeks.

How long did it take for the plant to grow—five years or six weeks? The answer is five years. During these five years, the plant develops penetrating roots, thus gaining the strength needed to support the height to which the tree will grow in the future. But we cannot see this growth externally. What if the farmer, disillusioned by the absence of any visible result, stops nurturing the seed? There will be no bamboo trees. It is his faith, patience and enthusiasm that eventually crowns his efforts with success.

Similarly, though we may not notice any palpable sign of spiritual growth, Amma is patiently and lovingly nurturing us. She knows that her children will grow, if not today, tomorrow. Because the water and fertilizer are from Amma, there is no doubt that her efforts will bear fruit.

Amma has lit a lamp of love inside each one of our hearts. Let us protect this flame carefully. The light of this 'eternal lamp' will illumine our path and help us overcome obstacles and pitfalls. May Amma bless us all so that we can preserve her light and love in our hearts forever. ॐ

22

"No devotee of mine is ever lost!"

Bri. Chinmayamrita Chaitanya

Lord Krishna declares, "Even if the worst sinners worship me with one-pointed devotion, they are to be considered righteous, for they have resolved properly" (*Bhagavad Gita*, 9.30). Such is the potency of devotion that the sinner becomes saintly.

The classical examples of this are Angulimala and Valmiki. Before they turned over a new leaf, both robbed and killed. After cultivating exclusive devotion towards God, they became paragons of virtue.

Krishna then asks Arjuna to "declare boldly that no devotee of mine is ever lost" (9.31).

Why did the Lord not say so himself? Why did he ask Arjuna to do so? If Arjuna, a devotee, were to declare it, God will definitely fulfil his words, for the Lord will never allow the words of his devotees to prove untrue. During the Mahabharata War, the Lord had taken a vow not to use any weapon. But when Bhishma, a true devotee of Krishna, vowed either to kill Arjuna or to make the Lord use a weapon, Krishna immediately wielded the wheel of the chariot as a weapon in order to protect Arjuna and to fulfil Bhishma's words, even though it meant violating his own vow.

Similarly, for Amma, her children are everything. She even says that her children are her God. Many years ago, a brahmacharini and I went to Mangalapuram for Amma's program. As Amma was about to leave after the program, both of us stood near the door to her room to see her off. As she was leaving right

after the program, we did not get any time to bathe. We were
dirty from seva, and our feet and clothes were soiled with mud.
When Amma saw us, she said, "Children, Amma wants to speak
to you. Both of you should get into the other vehicle."

Though we did not understand what she meant, we nodded.
While getting into the car, she turned to look at us and repeated,
"Both of you should get into the other vehicle." She then left for
a house visit. We, too, went for the house visit. There, Amma
repeated the same thing after the house visit. But we were so dull
headed that we still did not understand what Amma meant by "the
other vehicle." Another brahmacharini who heard what Amma
told us asked us to get into Amma's camper. We immediately
jumped into the spick and span camper, and dirtied it with mud!

After some time, Amma boarded the camper. Seeing her, one
of the brahmacharinis asked, wonderstruck, "Amma! Is this real
or a dream?"

Amma pinched her and asked, "What do you think?"

I told Amma that we had dirtied her camper. Amma replied,
"I like the dust of my children's feet."

I was stunned. I realized that for God, devotees are everything.
Amma is ever appreciative of her children.

Lord Krishna says that there are four kinds of devotees: *arta*,
artharthi, *jijnasu* and *jnani*. The arta is in pain and sorrow, and
begs God for relief. The artharthi prays for the fulfillment of
desires. The jijnasu is a seeker of knowledge; he worships the Lord
to gain wisdom. The jnani is a person of wisdom, i.e. he or she is
Self-illumined. Among the four kinds of devotees, Krishna says
that the jnani is dearest to him.

Whatever devotees aspire to gain, God tries to fulfill those
desires, and gradually raises them to a higher level. This can
clearly be seen with Amma, who is like an ever-flowing river of
love. Some use her. Some love her. Some abuse her. Some worship

her. Some do not even come near her. Like a river, Amma takes everyone and everything in her stride. Saint or sinner, rich or poor, intelligent or ignorant, Amma receives everyone equally.

God always protects devotees. Krishna goes one step further: he says that even if one is a sinner but has resolved to change and walk the path of *dharma* (righteousness), one will be redeemed, i.e. protected by the Lord. The doctor gives more attention to patients who require critical care. Similarly, Amma is more attentive towards people who require her attention.

I recall an incident that took place during one of Amma's North Indian tours years ago. A devotee forcibly brought his friend, who drank heavily and was a chain smoker, for Amma's darshan during her Mumbai program. After each bout of drinking, he would fight with his family members, disrupting the harmony at home. By the time this man reached Amma, he was drenched in cold sweat and his hands were trembling because he had not been able to drink or smoke for the last few hours. Further, he was anxious that Amma would not greet him lovingly, as she did others. When he appeared before Amma, she gently stroked his chest, caressed his cheeks, and gazed lovingly at him. Overwhelmed, he hugged Amma and started crying. Neither one of them said anything. After a long darshan, Amma asked him to sit beside her. Sitting near her, the man became calm and composed, and felt no symptom of alcohol or tobacco withdrawal. After some time, he got up and went home.

He returned the next day with his family. This time when he went for darshan, Amma told him, "Amma knows that it's very difficult for you to quit smoking and drinking. But don't worry. Everything will be fine."

He was surprised as he had not told Amma anything about his addictions. Once again, he broke down crying. He said, "O Amma, while I am with you, I can control my mind. But when you leave, it will be very hard for me to stay away from my bad habits."

Amma replied, "Son, don't worry. There is Devi Bhava darshan tomorrow. Amma will give you a mantra then. It will help you to control your urge to drink or smoke."

After he received a mantra from Amma, he was gradually able to overcome his urge to drink and smoke.

There are countless incidents like this. In his case, Amma gave him a mantra. In other cases, Amma gives people *kasturi* pills, which work wonders for them, but only because of Amma's *sankalpa* (divine resolve).

Once, there was a preacher living opposite a prostitute. Every day, he would count the number of people visiting the prostitute and would constantly brood over her sinful activities.

As for the prostitute, she was always thinking about God, regretting her ways, and begging pardon from God.

When she died, she reached Vaikuntha, the abode of Lord Vishnu, whereas when the preacher died, he went to hell, because his mind was constantly dwelling on the prostitute's sins.

What matters is not what others do but whether or not we are connected to God. Are we open to Amma irrespective of what we do? If we are, then Amma will take care of everything.

Amma has spoken about how some children who came to her during their childhood stopped coming during their adolescence, when they became more interested in their friends and group activities. But they eventually returned to Amma because she had sown in them the seeds of spirituality, devotion and love when they were young. Such is the potency of Amma's grace and compassion. She says that she sows the seed of spirituality in each and every person who comes to her, even once; at the right time, the seed will sprout. Who other than Amma can do this?

The following incident happened in Amrita Vidyalayam, Delhi. The husband of one of the school staff had a stroke. He was admitted to the intensive care unit (ICU) of a hospital, where he became paralyzed and lost his voice totally. The doctors told his wife that they might not be able to save him; even if he were saved, he might remain in a vegetative state for the rest of his life. His wife was distraught. She came crying to me: "Madam, please visit my husband! I have the firm faith that Amma will do something through you."

Praying to Amma with all my heart, I went to see her husband. Since one cannot spend much time in the ICU, I chanted *"Aum amriteshwaryai namah"* 18 times and left. I gave his wife an archana book and asked her to chant Amma's *Ashtottaram* (108 attributes) as often as she could, and to chant 'Aum amriteshwaryai namah' as much as possible. She prayed to Amma intensely. To the doctors' surprise, her husband showed signs of progress. Within a few months, he recovered by 70 – 80%.

When Krishna spoke about how even the worst sinners should be considered righteous if they resolve properly, he added one condition: *ananya bhakti*, i.e. unbroken or one-pointed devotion for God. This effectively means that the devotee should perceive the Lord in each and every being.

But Amma does not place such stringent demands on her children. If we have even the slightest devotion, she is ready to help us. The following incident testifies to this.

Following Amma's instructions, all the Amrita Vidyalayams conduct *Sanskriti Puja* on Guru Purnima.[9] During this puja, children worship their parents as Shiva and Shakti. Amma says that parents, especially the mother, are the child's first Gurus. Children perform *pada puja* (ceremonial washing of their feet), garland them, offer *dhupam, dipam, karpuram* and *naivedyam*

---

[9] The full moon (*'purnima'*) day in the Hindu month of *Ashadha* (June – July) in which disciples honor the Guru; also, the birthday of Sage Vyasa, compiler of the Vedas, and author of the Puranas, *Brahmasutras, Mahabharata* and the *Shrimad Bhagavatam.*

(incense, light, fire and food respectively), and dedicate an archana (chanting of the Lord's names) to their parents. Once, one of the fathers who sat for the puja began to recall how he had ill-treated his mother, neglected her for a long time, and always considered her a burden. When his child was doing puja to him, his mind became filled with remorse and he started crying, recalling how much pain his mother had taken to bring him up.

After the puja ended, he went straight to his mother, made her sit on a chair, sat down at her feet, and did the same puja to her. When his mother asked, "Son, what happened?" he tearfully told her how his child had worshipped him that day in school as part of the Guru Purnima observances, how he had been so touched by it, and how the puja had made him remember how badly he had treated her. He pleaded, "O mother, please forgive me."

Later, the father sent the school a letter, in which he narrated what had happened. Though he was not a devotee of Amma and was only connected to her through the school, by resolving rightly, Amma had showered her blessings on him. She helped him repent and atone for his mistakes.

Amma has assumed the form of a mother. A normal mother has unconditional love towards her child. Amma's love is that of Jagajjanani (Mother of the Universe). Her boundless compassion flows towards all her children

It is impossible to describe Amma's glory. To paraphrase a verse from the *Shiva Mahimna Stotra* (Hymn in Praise of Lord Shiva), even if one took a mountain of ink, the dark ocean as the ink-pot, a branch of a heavenly tree as the pen, and the earth as parchment, and even if Goddess Saraswati wrote forever, even then, O Amma, one would not be able to extol you sufficiently.

May Amma bless all of us with one-pointed devotion.

23

Eluding Maya
Br. Ramanandamrita Chaitanya

More than a decade ago, I was standing beside Amma during darshan when a devotee came with a long letter that he wanted translated to Amma. The letter began this way: "My cousin has pancreatic cancer..." To ensure I translated all the words properly into Malayalam, I consulted a Malayalam dictionary on my phone before translating. When I finished, Amma looked at me as if I were crazy and said, "I don't understand Hindi!" Amma then asked one of the darshan assistants to translate. She read the letter and told Amma that the man's 'cousin' had 'pancreatic cancer' (saying both terms in English, whereas I had used the Malayalam words). Amma then turned to me and said, "Only if you translate like that can I understand."

I learnt an important lesson from this incident. As a translator, my job was to help Amma understand whatever question or problem the person coming for darshan had. Instead, I had tried to impress Amma with my Malayalam vocabulary and lost track of the goal. This is how it is with much of life. We get so caught up with our concerns that we miss the bigger picture of life.

The scriptures declare,

brahma satyam jagat mithya iti evam rupah vinishcayah

The Supreme alone is true. Creation is unreal. This is a firm conviction. (*Vivekachudamani*, 20)

Here, mithya (illusory) refers to what obscures the Truth or draws us away from it. Sanatana Dharma considers everything a part of the Supreme. Creation is a manifestation of the Creator.

The truth is that everyone, with the exception of *jnanis* (knowers of the Truth) like Amma, are trapped in the web of illusion. Lord Krishna says as much and also tells us how we may move from untruth to Truth.

> *daivi hyesha gunamayi mama maya duratyaya*
> *mameva ye prapadyante mayametam taranti te*

> Maya, my divine spell, which comprises the three *gunas (attributes)*, is difficult to overcome. But one who takes refuge in me can certainly transcend it. (*Bhagavad Gita*, 7.14)

Maya is considered the Divine Mother. The *Lalita Sahasranama* (1,000 names of the Divine Mother) hails Devi as Maya (mantra 716). This power of cosmic illusion is also known as Maya-shakti.

There are different texts that discuss creation and the nature of creation. The *Brihadaranyaka Upanishad* mentions that nothing existed. Here nothingness refers to the unmanifest state of Brahman, the Supreme. Its power of manifestation is Maya or Shakti, which has three *gunas* (attributes): *sattva, rajas* and *tamas*—which may be loosely translated as the qualities of goodness or harmony, action or passion, and lethargy or destruction respectively. Brahman in its manifest form is also known as *mula-prakriti* (fundamental matter), and from it evolved the *panca-bhutas* (five basic elements)—space, air, fire, water and earth. Through the process known as *pancikarana*, these subtle elements became gross. The play of the three gunas in each of the five basic elements gave rise to the 24 principles of creation—*mahat* (great principle), *buddhi* (intelligence), *ahamkara* (ego), *manas* (mind), five *pancendriyas* (sense organs), five *karmendriyas* (organs of action), five *tanmatras* (subtle elements), and five *mahabhutas* (gross elements).

According to the Big Bang theory, energy was completely dormant initially. The built-up energy caused a big bang. In a similar vein, the *Aitareya Upanishad* says the one became many in accordance with the resolve of the Supreme. Through this process evolved the elements of creation.

Amma points out how the incarnations of Lord Vishnu depict evolution. The first incarnation was *matsya* (fish), an aquatic being. This was followed by *kurma* (turtle), an amphibian. The succeeding incarnations were land creatures: *varaha* (boar), Narasimha (half lion, half man), Vamana, a dwarf, and Lord Rama and Lord Krishna.

According to the law of the conservation of energy, energy is neither created nor destroyed. It only changes form, but the net sum of energy in creation remains constant. Our concept of the Supreme is similar. Nirguna Brahman is the Supreme without attributes—formless and changeless. Saguna Brahman is the Supreme with attributes, and therefore assumes forms. Both, though, are Brahman.

One may well ask, "I experience everything in creation. I can see it, touch it and feel it. How then can it be mithya (illusory)?

Amma says,

> Mithya only means 'changing.' It doesn't mean that it is non-existent; it means that it is not permanent. If rice is ground, it becomes powder, which transforms into edibles and then into excreta. There is only transformation.
> The object is still there. Similarly, there is no change in Brahman, the Absolute, whereas there is change in the

world. Brahman alone is the Truth, the world is illusory. To understand Maya, Brahman and such principles is very difficult. (*Awaken, Children*, Vol 1, 242)

It is difficult to understand Maya with the intellect and mind because the mind is itself a product of Maya.

Some years ago, during a retreat in North America, a devotee came to me and said that Amma had given him a spiritual name the day before; he wanted to know its meaning. When I asked him for the name, he said 'Anantate.' What an unusual name, I thought. I did not want to trouble Amma by asking her about it. Another devotee standing next to me said, "Isn't it Devi's name? It's in the bhajan *'Anantamayi Patarunnorakashame'*— *"ammayille enikkammayille parayu parayu anantate."* When I checked the English bhajan books, I saw that the word was 'anandame,' not 'anantate.' But in the Malayalam book, the word was 'anantate.' In any case, I could not see how 'anantate' could be a name. I decided to use my knowledge of Sanskrit to give this devotee an explanation for the name. In Sanskrit, 'ananta' means endless or expansive. 'Te' means 'your.' By this logic, 'anantate' means 'your endless / expansive.' But endless what? I asked him what his last name was. "Bottoms," he said. "Your expansive bottom?" I looked him up and down. His bottom looked scrawny!

I decided to ask Amma, who remembered that the man had come for darshan the day before. However, she denied having given him a spiritual name. But the devotee insisted that he had received the name during darshan. I told Amma that he said she had given him the name 'Anantate.' Hearing this, Amma pulled my ears sharply and said, "I told him 'Another Day.'"

Amma had asked him to come back on another day! We had made much ado about nothing. That is also what happens with Maya casts her spell on us. We exert ourselves mentally and intellect, but no matter what, we will never be able to figure it out because Maya is that which is not.

Amma never tells us to reject the world because it is Maya; all we need to do is to have the right understanding when we interact with it, i.e. to focus on the eternal while living amidst the ephemeral.

Say we need to reach Kochi Airport. We need to travel along the highway leading there. Is the highway our destination? No. Likewise, there are many distractions on the way. Nevertheless, we remain focused on our destination: the airport.

Every object in the world has elements that change. But each object also has a defining property or characteristic that remains constant. It is enough if we focus on that constant. Take a car, for example. We may or may not like its color, make, brand, size or type of tires. If we are fixated on these details, we are likely to become dissatisfied easily. But if we focus on the car itself and its purpose, we will not.

A few years ago at the San Ramon Ashram, the white Lexus that usually takes Amma to and from the hall met with a small accident. Another car was needed. A small blue Honda Accord was cleaned and used to drive Amma back to the house. When she walked into the house, a devotee asked her, "Was the drive okay?"

Amma found that question unusual and wondered why the devotee was asking about it; after all, it was a short drive. The devotee pointed out that Amma had come in a smaller car. With a look of surprise, Amma looked at the blue Honda and asked, "Isn't this the car Amma always comes in?"

For Amma, whether it is a Lexus or Honda, luxurious or non-luxurious, big or small, or white or blue does not make a difference. She is identified with the constant among the variables, in this case, the car.

This does not mean that cars are permanent. At a higher level, road transportation is the constant, and cars, buses and trains are variables. At a yet higher level, transportation is the constant whereas land, air and sea travel are the variables. If we thus keep moving 'higher,' we will realize that there is only one constant in this changing universe of names and forms: Brahman. Everything else is mithya.

In *Tattva Bodha*, Sri Shankara says that the reflection of the Supreme in every individual is *jiva*, and its reflection in the creation is *Ishwara* (God). The ego makes the jiva feel separate from the Supreme, and ignorance makes Ishwara seem different from the Absolute. Ego and ignorance create Maya.

Sri Shankara says that one needs certain qualities to realize the Truth: *viveka* (discernment), *vairagya* (dispassion), *shat-sampatti* (six virtues) and *mumukshutva* (intense desire for spiritual liberation). The six virtues are *shama* (control of mind), *dama* (control of senses), *uparati* (equanimity), *titiksha* (forbearance), *shraddha* (one-pointedness) and *samadhana* (acceptance and mental composure).

Amma says that spiritual aspirants need shraddha, *bhakti* (devotion and dedication) and *vishvas* (faith) to overcome hurdles on the spiritual path.

The easiest way to overcome the ego and to get rid of ignorance is to seek and become eligible for the Guru's grace. To become deserving, we need to have *sharanagati* (surrender).

We may feel there is Maya even around *mahatmas* (spiritually illumined souls) like Amma. Here, we need to ask ourselves if they are the ones who cast the spell of Maya or if it is our mind that is sunk in delusion.

In the *Bhagavad Gita*, Lord Krishna says,

naham prakashah sarvasya yoga-maya-samavrtah
mudho'yam nabhijananti loko mam-ajam-avyayam

Veiled as I am by Yogamaya, not everyone perceives
me. The ignorant do not know that I am birthless and
changeless. (7.25)

Not everything that happens around Amma may please our ego.
During one bhajan recording, I was playing the harmonium. I
might have made a mistake that disturbed Amma's mood, because
she asked me to leave and asked someone else to play instead. I
could have chosen to feel dejected and complained to Amma that
my ego had been hurt. Or I could have focused on Amma instead
of what happened to me. I humbly pray to her that I am always
able to choose the latter option in such situations.

In 2007, Amma suddenly told me to do a PhD in the US. She
said that she wants brahmacharis who were qualified enough to
manage Amrita University in the future. Fast forward to 2008: I
knew that, being alone in the US, I could go astray with no one
to monitor me. I decided to adopt a few principles that would
help me keep my focus on the path.

The first was what I called 'cell phone sadhana;' I wanted to
see my mobile phone as a reminder of my connection to Amma,
who could call me any time. If she calls me and asks, "What are
you doing?" would I be able to tell her what I was doing without
any hesitation or guilt? If I can, then it is fine to continue what I
was doing. If not, I should reconsider my actions.

The second principle was inspired by Amma. Though she
has travelled to so many countries for more than three decades,
Amma has never gone sightseeing. Once, during a drive, when
I pointed out a beautiful sight, Amma refused to look out of the
window. She said that it would remind her that her children in

Amritapuri cannot see this sight; how can she enjoy it when her children cannot? I decided I, too, would not do any sightseeing. Let me confess that I did visit a few places of natural beauty. But to justify the visit, I would meditate or do archana there so as to spiritualize the visit. In case Amma asked, I could tell her that I had done some sadhana there.

In 2013, Amma asked me to take care of the Boston ashram as well. When I first went there, a devotee couple accommodated me. They wanted to take me somewhere. Even when I told them that I do not sightsee as a matter of principle, they insisted on driving me through Boston City. Seeing their sincerity, I gave in.

It was April 15th, 2013, the day of the Boston Marathon. The city was very crowded. The couple suggested that we visit the science museum in the city, as it was a place of learning and that Amma would not mind my going there. Even though I did not want to go, it is not in my nature to refuse anyone sternly. I ended up going to the museum with them. I was so racked with guilt. I thought, "What if Amma calls me now? How can I justify this as a spiritual experience?"

My mind became creative. When we went to the math section, I told myself that spirituality was also like math, as it involved figuring out what dharma is and what adharma is. In the physics section, I learnt about the physics behind the law of karma. The life sciences exhibits taught me that there is no meaning in being attached to the body; it is lifeless without soul. In this way, I tried to rationalize what I was doing.

Suddenly, there was a commotion. Police officers told us to leave. I learnt that, at around 2:55 p.m., there had been twin bomb blasts at the finishing point of the Boston Marathon, which was less than a mile from where I was standing.

While leaving, I realized that I had resisted sightseeing for my first five years in the US. But the first time I went sightseeing, there had been two bomb blasts less than a mile away from me. I felt guilty.

As we were driving back, my phone rang. I looked at my phone; it was an Indian number! Amma's voice came on. "Where are you now?"

I did not have the guts to tell her the truth, but I did not lie either. I said that I was on my way to the Boston Ashram. She asked, "Did you hear about the bomb blast?" I thought, I did not have to hear *about* it; I was where I could literally hear the blasts.

The phone call reminded me that Amma is always watching me. When I could not maintain a vow I had taken, Amma had intervened to remind me about it.

May we all become worthy of Amma's grace. May she hold our hands and guide us to the Supreme. ೭ৎৡৰ

24

But for Her Grace

Br. Omkaramrita Chaitanya

We are all blessed to be born in the era of a great master like Amma. To live in her presence is to experience spiritual life truly. No spiritual text can teach us what we can learn from the personal guidance of a Guru. Whatever she tells us to do is for our own spiritual growth. By obeying her, we can attain peace and solace.

My main area of seva in the ashram has been in the kitchen, and it is through this seva that Amma has guided me. She often says, "nothing is insignificant," and validates it through her actions. Once, there was a pile of chopped wood out in the open behind the kitchen. Because of my negligence, I did not shift the firewood to a dry place before the rains fell, and it became wet. A few days later, Amma saw the wet firewood and personally moved the whole pile to a shelter. This was Amma 'leading by example.'

I am particular about keeping the kitchen clean, but would ask the workers to do so. One day, Amma came into the kitchen and went directly to the vegetable racks. Seeing how dirty the racks were, she took a few rags and started cleaning them. After cleaning them, Amma started putting the vegetables back methodically. She then went to where the vessels were being washed. The workers were not washing the big vessels properly. Amma showed them how to brush away the dirt on the edges completely, and explained why they had to be cleaned.

When Amma does something and then tells you why, you learn the lesson well. After this incident, the kitchen workers started cleaning the vessels with more sincerity and alertness. This is why Amma is such an inspirational leader. Instead of just giving instructions, she teaches by showing us how to do things in a better way, and with more sincerity and alertness. This is why it is said that Amma's life itself is her message.

Before serving in the Amritapuri kitchen, I was at the Ettimadai (Coimbatore) campus of Amrita University. There, I went through a phase when I was not as vigilant as I needed to be. I became lax in my spiritual practices and even considered leading a worldly life instead. Unable to overcome the wavering in my mind, I decided to confide in Amma.

I went to Amritapuri and opened up to Amma, who graciously gave me a patient hearing. Then, giving me a loving hug, she said, "Son, you unburdened your heart completely to me. Now, may grace guide you to make the right decision." That gave me such a huge relief, and I felt that all my confusion had vanished completely. I became sure that I did not wish to lead a worldly life but wanted to rededicate the rest of my life to serving Amma wholeheartedly. This experience made me realize that however great a problem may be, if we confide in Amma, it will cease to trouble us.

We might think, if Amma knows everything, then why express our problems to her? Yes, she is all-knowing. But our conviction is not complete. When we open up to Amma, we become one with her in those moments. That inner connectedness becomes a conduit for the flow of her grace, which will protect us from all perils.

After this incident, with Amma's permission, I moved from Ettimadai to Amritapuri, where she assigned me the responsibility of running the ashram kitchen.

Amma taught me each and every aspect of managing the ashram kitchen—making tea and curry, cooking rice, studying the market, bargaining with vendors to get the best prices...

Earlier, the practice in the kitchen was to make a few kettles of tea with milk. Sometimes, only a third of the tea would be consumed, especially on the mornings after Devi Bhava. As a result, much of the tea would be wasted. Amma asked me to prepare black tea and to keep the boiled milk separately. Later, depending on the requirements, we could mix the two. If there were any milk left, we could use it to make yogurt. This ensured that nothing was wasted.

When it came to rice, Amma told us to choose a variety of grain that yields a larger quantity when cooked as well as one that had a longer shelf life. Taking her advice to heart, I bought four varieties of grains and boiled an equal quantity of each in different vessels. I weighed them all and took them to Amma, thinking that she would choose the one that weighed the most. I also imagined that she would express appreciation for my thoroughness.

But Amma corrected my understanding. She said that for parboiled rice, what matters is not the weight but quantity. The best-quality grains become larger when cooked.

She did not stop there. She asked me to cook one kilogram of each variety and to study how many people could be fed. She also asked me to consider different categories of consumers: students, workers, staff, ashram residents, etc. Amma also told me to make *kanji* (rice gruel) in the same way and to compare consumption among the different categories of consumers. Similarly, Amma taught me how to observe and take into account various aspects of cooking while making curries, *dosa*, *idli*, *uppuma* and other items. I consider myself immensely blessed to have received so much personal guidance from Amma, who took the time to do so amidst her hectic schedule.

One day, Amma telephoned me and asked for some rice, vegetables and other items. I collected the required items and rushed to her room. When I arrived, Amma told me that she was going to cook. She washed the rice, rinsed and chopped the vegetables, and cooked them in two separate vessels, adding the necessary ingredients. The whole time, she was talking to me. At one point, she stopped speaking. From the aroma, she knew that the food was well-cooked and ready to serve. I tasted what Amma had made: it was delicious! Everything was just right: how much they had been boiled, the quantity of salt and other ingredients, etc. Without removing the lids midway to check or taste it, Amma knew when they were ready just from the smell. She said that people of an older generation used to be so thorough and precise that their skills were instinctive.

Amma not only taught me cooking, she also taught me the fundamentals of purchasing. For every item, I was to compare prices from some 10 different places. In this way, we got the best deals. For vegetables, Amma asked me to go to the farms where they are sourced instead of buying them from markets. This way, we would get fresher and cheaper vegetables. Amma's practicality, sharp business sense and market knowledge are truly astonishing. With her guidance, I cultivated more *shraddha* (alertness).

Amritavarsham50, Amma's 50th birthday celebration, was a four-day affair in which devotees from all parts of the world participated. We had to make dining arrangements for an average of half a million people daily. This included arranging for sufficient plates for all the meals. After discussing the matter, the team responsible for buying paper plates felt that we should order about four million paper plates.

When we told Amma about this, she called the team for a meeting in her room. She listened intently to us as we explained how we had arrived at that number. Then she said, "It would be a crime against nature to buy four million paper plates. So many trees would have to be cut down to make so many paper plates. It will also generate so much waste that would be a burden on nature. Let's buy steel plates instead. They can be washed and reused. After the birthday, we can send the plates to our various university campuses, hospitals, branch ashrams and schools, where plates are needed."

Amma asked me to find out about the number of plates that each institution and branch ashram needed. She also asked me to check the prices of different types and sizes of plates. After many inquiries, I went to Amma with a sample plate cost Rs.30 for her approval. She said, "Son, it's good but feels a bit too heavy. Look for lighter plates that are cheaper but of higher quality."

Two days later, a sales executive from a plate making company called to tell me about their product. From the description, I felt that it would fit our requirements. I obtained a sample and showed it to Amma, who approved it instantly. We bought 50,000 plates for a quarter of the amount we would have spent on paper plates. In addition, we collected another 50,000 plates from our various institutions. We were able to serve everyone with these plates. To this day, those plates are still in use in Amritapuri and our branch ashrams.

We had also projected a requirement of about 80,000 liters of milk. I contacted many companies to check if they could supply such a large quantity. One company from Tamil Nadu agreed to supply what we needed at a reasonable price. It also offered to supply other dairy products at no additional cost. Pleased with this offer, I went to tell Amma about it.

Amma said that the milk supplier should be certified by the government, and that we should finalize the deal only after confirming this. I contacted the company and asked for proof of government certification. It sent a copy of the certificate, but

Amma wanted to see the original. As the company was unable to do so, the deal was called off.

The only option left was to go with Milma, a well-known Kerala Government company. Though it could not offer us the same rates as the company from Tamil Nadu, the terms it offered were still favorable. Milma would send a milk tanker to the venue from 4 a.m. – 11 a.m. and from 3 p.m. – 7 p.m. We could take as much as we needed, and would be charged only for what we took.

Our earlier estimates proved wrong. There were many shops around the venue, and many people patronized these shops. We also used milk powder in addition to what we bought from Milma. In the end, we did not buy as much milk as we had originally projected. By following Amma's instructions, we not only saved money but also avoided a huge wastage.

A year later, when the tsunami lashed the South Indian coast, Alappad village, where Amritapuri is situated, was also badly affected. About 150 people from this village died. Amma started relief activities immediately by arranging dinner for the victims. The ashram fed all the villagers thrice daily for months together. I gained immense satisfaction in playing my part in this seva. In addition, I had to attend to other routine responsibilities, such as arranging food for ashram residents, university students, marriages that took place in the ashram, etc. For all these, Amma guided me directly.

After some years, I gained considerable experience in cooking for many events. I thought I knew enough and became half-hearted about seeking guidance from Amma, only doing so as a mere formality. Amma knows when and how to cut us down to size.

In 2013, *Amritavarsham60*, Amma's 60th birthday celebration, was held at the Amritapuri campus of Amrita University. It was a three-day event. On the first day, by 10 am, all the dishes for lunch had been cooked. All that needed to be done was to ensure that they were sent to the various distribution counters. Confident that this would be done without a hitch, I went to my room to take a break. I fell asleep. After some time, someone called me hurriedly and said that the rice was almost over, and that many people had not eaten yet.

I rushed into the kitchen. Usually, there are many cooking vessels filled with boiled water. All one has to do is to add grains, and cooked rice would be ready in 10 or 15 minutes. To my dismay, none of the cooking vessels were there; someone had taken them away without my knowledge. I also usually set aside some half-cooked rice and vegetables for such eventualities. I had not done so that day.

Retrieving the vessels, filling them with water, boiling it and cooking rice — the whole process took a few hours. Many devotees who could not wait so long left without eating.

I felt completely dejected. I went to Amma and sat next to her. She was talking to other people and did not spare me a glance. She told them that she was feeling very sad that many devotees had left without eating. Then, without even looking at me, she returned to her room. I became upset, went to my room and cried a lot.

After two days, Amma called me on the phone and consoled me. She said, "Many devotees were sad when they didn't get prasad that day. You should also understand the sorrow they felt. That's why I didn't talk to you then. Unlike the previous years, you didn't check with me on kitchen matters this year. That's why all these things happened. May divine grace protect you." Saying so, she hung up.

After this experience, I realized that I cannot do anything on my own. But if Amma is with me, there is nothing I cannot do.

Amma says that we should become conduits for divine grace. Water from a tank flows smoothly through a pipe because it is hollow inside. Likewise, if our mind is free of selfish desires, we will also become a conduit for divine grace. Water always flows to a lower level. This means that we need to be humble if we want to receive grace.

Vyadha, the butcher (mentioned in the *Bhagavata Purana*), and the *gopis* (milkmaids) of Vrindavan all did humble jobs. Yet, they attained the highest spiritual state because all their actions were done with intense remembrance of Lord Krishna. Arjuna's fighting became an offering unto God because he fought with an attitude of surrender to the Lord.

Referring to the ashram, Amma once said, "The soil here has been soaked in Amma's tears. It has been scorched by fiery embers. Facing much opposition, criticism and hostility, and overcoming them all, Amma has built this ashram. Its foundations are love and sacrifice."

The work that Amma gives us is an opportunity to purify ourselves so that we may become deserving of grace. It does not matter what we do, but how we do it; it is the attitude behind our actions that counts. With the right attitude, work becomes worship. When we act with an attitude of surrender, our karma becomes karma yoga. May we all be able to do our work as an offering to our beloved Amma. ༺༻

25

Her Protection
Bri. Nirmuktamrita Chaitanya

The *Bhagavad Gita* is the crystallized essence of all the scriptures.
Its greatness is beyond description. Lord Krishna himself extols
the greatness of this sacred text in its final chapter:

> He who, with supreme love for me, teaches this supreme
> and sublime secret to my devotees shall doubtless come to
> me.
> No one else serves me more dearly than he; nor shall
> there be another on earth dearer to me than he.
> He who studies this sacred dialogue worships me
> through the sacrifice of knowledge; this is my conviction.
> He who hears this with utmost faith and with no malice
> whatsoever shall be liberated from sin and attain the
> blessed worlds of the morally upright. (18. 68 – 71)

Though dispensed to Arjuna in the battlefield of Kurukshetra, the
Lord's advice is meant for all Arjunas—those in need of spiritual
solace and guidance—for all times. But to benefit from his advice,
the seeker must have the maturity and aptitude to learn different
ways to reach the ultimate knowledge.

In the ninth chapter, Lord Krishna hails the message of
the *Gita* as the supreme science, secret and purifier (*"rajavidya
rajaguhyam pavitramidamuttamam"*) (9.2). Of all knowledge, he
is the knowledge of the Self (10. 32). It is the supreme secret

because the wicked, the atheists and the indifferent will find this knowledge difficult to understand. The Lord offers the most reassuring promise:

kshipram bhavati dharmatma shashvacchantim nigacchati
kaunteya pratijanihi na me bhaktah pranashyati

Soon he becomes a noble soul and certainly attains lasting peace. O Arjuna, declare boldly that no devotee of mine is ever lost. (*Bhagavad Gita*, 9.31)

Who qualifies as a devotee? What is devotion? Devotion is love for God. It is the dissolution of the mind in God. This happens when one forgets the lower self. Sri Shankara says, *"Svasvar-upanusandhanam bhaktirityabhidhiyate"*—"Devotion is inquiry into one's own Self." (*Vivekachudamani*, 31)

Remembrance of God is like a seed that is sown. It produces many fruits. *Ananya bhakti*, exclusive devotion, is like a steady and unbroken stream of oil flowing downwards. In an ideal devotee, we can see purity of thoughts, feelings and emotions. Amma says, "Children, develop a childlike heart."

The Lord praises the devotee and devotion in chapter nine and in the preceding and following chapters. He says that he dwells in the devotee and that the devotee dwells in him. Those who constantly meditate on him as not separate from other beings worship him in all beings. To them, he grants full protection and fulfills all their needs. Such devotees eventually attain him, the supreme being. The one and only way to liberation is through *samyak jnana* (true knowledge), the realization that *'vasudeva sarvamiti'*—God pervades the whole world.

The Lord speaks about the four types of devotees: the distressed; the seeker of knowledge; the seeker of enjoyment, wealth and fame; and the knower of the Truth. The ideal devotee, discussed earlier, belongs to the last category of devotees. As Arjuna listens to the Lord's teachings, many doubts arise in his mind. We may also have such doubts. For example, is everyone equal before God? Or does God discriminate? The Lord clears these doubts in verses 29 – 31:

> I am the same to all beings. There is no one hateful or dear to me. But those who devoutly worship me abide in me, and I, too, am in them.
> If even the worst sinner worships me with exclusive devotion, he, too, should be considered righteous, for he has rightly resolved.
> O Arjuna, he soon becomes virtuous and attains lasting peace. Know for sure that my devotee will never be ruined.

Amma says, "Those who have insured their cars and homes need not fear." Likewise, those who have surrendered to God need not fear. When Lord Krishna says, "my devotee will never be ruined," it is a promise that he will take care of and protect us.

I remember the very first time I saw Amma, in 1994. Every week thereafter, I would go to the Kaimanam Ashram for bhajans. I did not know anyone there. One day, the bhajans ended late. I waited by the road for a bus. As I have limited vision, I cannot read the bus boards or even distinguish vehicles from afar. Because of that, I would flag any vehicle as soon as I saw its headlights, mistaking it for a bus. Only when it came near would I realize that it was a lorry, for example. After some time, I stopped flagging vehicles and thought, "Let Amma send me a vehicle."

After a while, a bus stopped for me. It was a Limited Stop Bus, which never stops at bus stands like the one at which I was waiting. I was surprised. I got into the bus and sat down. I had a government issued blind pass, which entitled me to free rides. The conductor approached me and said, "Sister, where are you going?" I showed him the pass and told him where I was going. As we were about to reach my stop, he said, "Sister, it's really late. Do not walk back all alone. Let me get you an auto-rickshaw." He then hailed an auto-rickshaw for me.

A week later, I met a family that later became residents of the Amritapuri Ashram. They offered to pick me up and drop me off in their car. So, I started traveling with them.

Once, they were unable to go to the ashram. So, I waited by the roadside again, hoping to catch a bus. After a while, a bus came and stopped for me, even though I had not flagged it. I boarded. I heard a voice behind me, "Sister, do you remember me?" I turned around. It was the conductor who had flagged an auto-rickshaw for me! He kindly did so again.

After this incident, I met a family of devotees living near my home. That family also had a car and they invited me to travel with them. Never again did I have to wait for a bus in the dark. This is how Amma took care of me, who had taken refuge in her. She is still taking care of me as if I were her golden child.

Amma is described as *"abrahma kita janani"*—"Mother of all, from Brahma to the lowliest insect" (*Lalita Sahasranama*, 285). Like the sun that shines upon all of creation, Amma showers her love equally on all, regardless of our shortcomings. The ultimate solution to all problems in life is to follow Amma's teachings and to change our attitude. If the merits gained from our previous lives guide us to a Guru, discernment will dawn within. A man trapped in a river inhabited by crocodiles escapes by catching hold of the overhanging branch of a tree growing on the river bank. Similarly, strong faith rooted in awareness will save us from pitfalls.

The Lord says that even the wicked will not perish if they worship him with unswerving faith. We might think, "That gives us the license to do any wicked deed!" Such an attitude is incorrect. Immoral acts and devotion to God are not compatible. When we truly start believing and worshipping God, we will abandon our wicked ways of life. When our devotion leaves no space for other thoughts, we will attain liberation in this very life.

Thousands of people who were immoral have been transformed after receiving Amma's darshan. Many have been able to give up smoking and drinking. This reminds me of an incident that another brahmacharini related to me.

There was a family who lived in Kasargod. The father was addicted to alcohol. One day, they traveled by car to see Amma. On the way, the man stopped at a bar and drank heavily. Somehow, they reached the ashram safely. The man told his wife, "Go for darshan and come back soon. I'm going to roam around and see the sights. If you're late, I'll leave without you!"

When his wife returned from darshan, she could not find her husband. As she anxiously searched for him, someone told her that he had been taken for darshan. When she saw him later, he was crying uncontrollably. He explained, "When I went for darshan, Amma asked me, 'Son are you drinking and beating up your wife and children daily?'" Her words totally transformed him and ushered peace into the family.

Amma's compassion is immeasurable. Each one of us must move closer to Amma. We must become instruments in her hands. We must become deserving of her grace. It is our ego that stands in the way. Amma constantly reminds us that she can only fill an empty pot. Let us pray to Amma to make us humble and deserving of her divine grace. ৩৯৯

GLOSSARY

acharya: one who consolidates the essentials of the scriptures, establishes them in tradition, and observes them in practice.

Advaita: not two; non-dual; philosophy that holds that the *jiva* (individual soul) and *jagat* (universe) are essentially one with *Brahman*, the Supreme Reality.

ahankara: from *'aham'*—'I' and *'kara'*—'maker.' Ego or the sense of a self that is separate from the rest of the universe.

ajnani: unlearned; ignorant.

Angulimala: 'finger garland.' The epithet of a brigand who cut off fingers from his victims and strung them in a garland that he wore. He underwent a transformation upon meeting the Buddha.

archana: chanting of the 108 or 1,000 names of a particular deity (e.g. *Lalita Sahasranama*).

Arjuna: great archer and one of the heroes of the *Mahabharata*. It is Arjuna whom Krishna addresses in the *Bhagavad Gita*.

artha: goal, wealth, substance; one of the four *purusharthas* (the goals of human endeavor).

artharthi: one of four types of devotees mentioned in the *Bhagavad Gita*, an *artharthi* is one who prays for wealth.

ashram: monastery. Amma defines it as a compound: *'a'*—'that' and *'shramam'*—'effort' (toward Self-realization).

Ashtottaram: litany of 108 attributes of a deity, divine incarnation or saint; short form of *ashtottara-shatam* (108) or *ashtottara-sha-ta-namavali* (108 names).

atma: Self or Soul.

avatar: from Sanskrit root *'ava–tarati'*—'to come down.' Divine Incarnation.

Bhagavad Gita: 'Song of the Lord,' it consists of 18 chapters of verses in which Lord Krishna advises Arjuna. The advice is given on the battlefield of Kurukshetra, just before the righteous Pandavas fight the unrighteous Kauravas. It is a practical guide to overcoming crises in one's personal or social life and is the essence of Vedic wisdom.

bhajan: devotional song or hymn in praise of God.

bhakti: devotion for God.

bhava: divine mood or attitude.

bhava darshan: see darshan.

bhava samadhi: state of devotional ecstasy.

Bhavatarini: one who frees the soul from the cycle of birth and death; a form of Goddess Kali.

Bhishma: patriarch of the Pandavas and Kauravas. Though he fought on the side of the Kauravas during the Mahabharata War, he was a champion of dharma and was sympathetic to the righteous Pandavas.

Brahma: Lord of Creation in the Hindu Trinity.

brahmachari: celibate male disciple who practices spiritual disciplines under a Guru's guidance. ('*Brahmacharini*' is the female equivalent.)

Brahman: ultimate truth beyond any attributes; the supreme reality underlying all life; the divine ground of existence.

Brahmsthanam: 'Abode of Brahman.' The name of the temples Amma consecrated in various parts of India and in Mauritius. The temple shrine features a unique four-faced idol that symbolizes the unity behind the diversity of divine forms.

Brahmin: member of the priestly caste.

buddhi: intellect; faculty of reasoning.

chapati: Indian flatbread.

chechi: 'older sister' in Malayalam.

chitta: the storehouse of mental impressions; sometimes used to refer to the heart.

Dakshinamurti: A form of Lord Shiva, facing the South, seated under a banyan tree, and surrounded by disciples. Considered the ultimate Guru, he communed with his disciples through silence.

dama: Self-control; self-restraint.

darshan: audience with a holy person or a vision of the Divine. Devi Bhava ('Divine Mood of Devi') refers to the state in which Amma reveals her oneness and identity with the Divine Mother. Krishna Bhava ('Divine Mood of Krishna') refers to the state in which Amma reveals her oneness and identity with Lord Krishna.

Devi: Goddess / Divine Mother.

dharana: 'Concentration.' Sixth of the 'eight limbs' ('*ashtanga*') of yoga described by Sage Patanjali is his *Yoga Sutras*.

dharma: 'that which upholds (creation).' Generally refers to the harmony of the universe, a righteous code of conduct, sacred duty or eternal law.

dhyana: meditation.

dhyana shloka: benedictory verse.

dosa: thin and savory pancake.

Dronacharya: Guru of both the Pandavas and Kauravas in the *Mahabharata*.

Dvaita: Duality; the philosophy that holds that God and the individual soul are two separate entities.

Ekalavya: character from the *Mahabharata*; a tribal prince famed for his skill in archery.

guna: one of three types of qualities, *viz.* sattva, rajas and tamas. Human beings express a combination of these qualities. Sattvic qualities are associated with calmness and wisdom, rajas with activity and restlessness, and tamas with dullness or apathy.

Guru: Spiritual teacher.

Guru Purnima: the full moon (*'purnima'*) day in the Hindu month of *Ashadha* (June – July) in which disciples honor the Guru; also, the birthday of Sage Vyasa, compiler of the Vedas, and author of the *Puranas, Brahmasutras, Mahabharata* and the *Shrimad Bhagavatam*.

Guruvayurappan: a form of Lord Vishnu, the Sustainer in the Hindu Trinity, worshipped mainly in Kerala.

hatha yoga: physical exercises or *asanas* designed to enhance one's overall well-being by toning the body and opening the various channels of the body to promote the free flow of energy; the science of *pranayama* (breath control), which includes other aspects of yoga, including asanas and *mudras* (esoteric hand gestures that express specific energies or powers).

idli: steamed cake made from a fermented batter of rice and lentils.

indriya: sense (organ).

ishvara: Lord; the inner ruler who guides from within.

japa: repeated chanting of a mantra.

jijnasa: desire to know (God).

jijnasu: one of four types of devotees mentioned in the *Bhagavad Gita*, one who longs to know God; one who is desirous of knowing something.

jiva: individual self or soul.

jnana: knowledge of the Truth.

jnani: one of four types of devotees mentioned in the *Bhagavad Gita*, one who knows God or has Self-knowledge.

Kali: Goddess of fearsome aspect; depicted as dark, wearing a garland of skulls, and a girdle of human hands; feminine of Kala (time).

kama: desire.

Kamsa: Lord Krishna's maternal uncle.

kanji: rice gruel.

karma: action; mental, verbal and physical activity; chain of effects produced by our actions.

karma kushalata: skill or dexterity in action.

karma yoga: the way of action, the path of selfless service.

Kauravas: the 101 children of King Dhritarashtra and Queen Gandhari, of whom the unrighteous Duryodhana was the eldest. The Kauravas were the enemies of their cousins, the virtuous Pandavas, whom they fought against in the Mahabharata War.

kripa: divine grace

Krishna: from '*krish*,' meaning 'to draw to oneself' or 'to remove sin;' principal incarnation of Lord Vishnu. He was born into a royal family but raised by foster parents, and lived as a cowherd boy in Vrindavan, where he was loved and worshipped by his devoted companions, the *gopis* (milkmaids) and *gopas* (cowherd boys). Krishna later established the city of Dvaraka. He was a friend and advisor to his cousins, the Pandavas, especially Arjuna, whom he served as charioteer during the Mahabharata War, and to whom he revealed his teachings as the *Bhagavad Gita*.

Kuchela: childhood friend of Lord Krishna.

Kurukshetra: battlefield where the war between the Pandavas and Kauravas was fought; also, a metaphor for the conflict between good and evil.

Lalita Sahasranama: litany of 1,000 names of Sri Lalita Devi, a form of the Goddess.
lila: divine play.

Mahabharata: ancient Indian epic that Sage Vyasa composed, depicting the war between the righteous Pandavas and the unrighteous Kauravas.
mahatma: 'great soul;' term used to describe one who has attained spiritual realization.
Malayalam: language spoken in the Indian state of Kerala.
Malayali: one whose mother-tongue is Malayalam.
manana: reflection on spiritual matters.
mantra: sound, syllable, word or words of spiritual content. Mantras are revelations to *rishis* that take place during their deep contemplation. Gurus initiate disciples and devotees into a specific mantra for their spiritual growth.
Matruvani: 'Voice of the Mother.' Magazine produced by the Mata Amritanandamayi Math, currently published in 17 languages.
Maya: Cosmic delusion, personified as a temptress. Illusion; appearance, as contrasted with reality; the creative power of the Lord; see Shakti.
mithya: changing, therefore impermanent. Also, illusory or untrue. According to Vedanta, the entire visible world is mithya.
moksha: spiritual liberation, i.e. release from the cycle of births and deaths.

nididhyasana: deep and repeated meditation on scriptural statements.

nirguna: without attributes (as opposed to saguna).

Om (Aum): primordial sound in the universe; the seed of creation. The cosmic sound, which can be heard in deep meditation; the Holy Word, taught in the Upanishads, which signifies Brahman, the divine ground of existence.

Om amriteshwaryai namah: 'Salutations to the Immortal Goddess.'

pada puja: ceremonial washing of the feet as a form of worship.

Pandavas: five sons of King Pandu, and cousins of Krishna.

papa: sin; wrongdoing.

paramatma: supreme Self.

Parashakti: supreme power, personified as the Goddess or Empress of the Universe.

Parvati: consort of Lord Shiva.

Patanjali Yoga Sutras: aphorisms composed by Sage Patanjali on the path to purification and transcendence of the mind.

payasam: sweet pudding.

prakriti: nature; primal matter.

prana: vital force.

pranava: the mystic syllable 'Aum' ('Om')

prasad: blessed offering or gift from a holy person or temple, often in the form of food.

prasada buddhi: the attitude of seeing everything one receives as a gift from God.

puja: ritualistic or ceremonial worship.

punya: spiritual merit.

purna: full or whole / spiritual fullness.

purusha: 'man' in Malayalam; 'supreme Self' in Sanskrit.

rajas: see guna.

Ramakrishna Paramahamsa: spiritual master (1836 – 1886) from West Bengal, hailed as the apostle of religious harmony. He generated a spiritual renaissance that continues to touch the lives of millions.

Ramana Maharshi: spiritual master (1879 – 1950) who lived in Tiruvannamalai, Tamil Nadu. He recommended Self-inquiry as the path to Liberation, though he approved of a variety of paths and spiritual practices.

Rama: divine hero of the *Ramayana*. An incarnation of Lord Vishnu, he is considered the ideal man of *dharma* and virtue. 'Ram' means 'to revel;' one who revels in himself; the principle of joy within; also, one who gladdens the hearts of others.

Ramayana: 24,000-verse epic poem on the life and times of Rama.

Ravana: powerful demon. Vishnu incarnated as Lord Rama to kill him and thereby restore harmony to the world.

rishi: seer to whom mantras are revealed in deep meditation.

Rukmini: chief consort of Lord Krishna.

sadhana: regimen of disciplined and dedicated spiritual practice that leads to the supreme goal of Self-realization.

saguna: with attributes (as opposed to nirguna).

samadhi: literally, 'cessation of all mental movements;' oneness with God; a transcendental state in which one loses all sense of individual identity; union with absolute reality; a state of intense concentration in which consciousness is completely unified.

samatva: even-mindedness or equanimity.

sambar: South Indian curry made from lentils and vegetables.

samsara: cycle of births and deaths; the world of flux; the wheel of birth, decay, death and rebirth.

samyama: 'holding together;' it combines the practices of *dharana*, *dhyana* and *samadhi*; also, self-control; one who is accomplished in this is a *samyami*.

Sanatana Dharma: literally, 'Eternal Religion' or 'Eternal Way of Life,' the original and traditional name for Hinduism.

sankalpa: divine resolve, usually used in association with *mahatmas*.

sannyasi: monk who has taken formal vows of renunciation (*sannyasa*); traditionally wears an ocher-colored robe, representing the burning away of all desires. The female equivalent is *sannyasini*.

Sanskrit: language of the oldest sacred text, the Rik Veda, and the other three Vedas; the language of most ancient Hindu scriptures.

Saraswati: Goddess of Learning and the Arts.

sari: traditional outer garment of Indian women consisting of a long, unstitched piece of cloth wrapped around the body.

sarvajnatva: omniscience

Satguru: 'true master.' All Satgurus are mahatmas, but not all mahatmas are Satgurus. The Satguru is one who, while still experiencing the bliss of the Self, chooses to come down to the level of ordinary people in order to help them grow spiritually.

satsang: communion with the Supreme Truth. Also, being in the company of *mahatmas*, studying scriptures, and listening to the enlightening talks of a *mahatma*; a meeting of people to listen to and/or discuss spiritual matters; a spiritual discourse.

sattva, sattvic: see guna.

Satyabhama: one of the consorts of Lord Krishna

seva: selfless service, the results of which are dedicated to God.

Shakti: personification of cosmic will and energy; strength; see Maya.

shama: control over the mind.

Shankaracharya: saint revered as a Guru and chief proponent of the Advaita (non-dual) philosophy.

sharanagati: total surrender to God or the Guru.

shastra: science; authoritative scriptural texts.

Shiva: worshipped as the first and the foremost in the lineage of Gurus, and as the formless substratum of the universe in relationship to Shakti. The Lord of Destruction in the Hindu Trinity.

shraddha: attentiveness; faith.

shravana: listening (to scriptural truths); often used in conjunction with *manana* and *nididhyasana*.

shruti: 'what is heard;' a reference to the Vedas, which were revealed to the rishis; also refers to pitch in music.

smriti: 'what is remembered;' refers to sacred Hindu texts that are attributed to rishis.

svadhyaya: daily or regular study of the scriptures; recitation of the Vedas and other scriptural texts.

svarup(a): one's own form or true nature.

Swami, Swamini: title of one who has taken the vow of *sannyasa* (see *sannyasi*). Swamini is the female equivalent.

tabla: a pair of Indian hand drums.

tamas, tamasic: see guna.

tapas: austerities, penance.

tulasi: holy basil.

Upanishad: portions of the Vedas dealing with Self-knowledge.

uppuma: pudding made from dry-roasted semolina; wheat farina.

vairagya: dispassion.

Valmiki: sage and author of the *Ramayana*.

vasana: latent tendency or subtle desire that manifests as thought, motive and action; subconscious impression gained from experience.

Vedas: most ancient of all scriptures, originating from God, the Vedas were not composed by any human author but were 'revealed' in deep meditation to the ancient seers. These sagely revelations came to be known as the Vedas, of which there are four: Rik, Yajus, Sama and Atharva.

Vidyalayam: school.

Vishnu: Lord of Sustenance in the Hindu Trinity.

Vishu: New Year in Kerala; celebrated at the end of the spring equinox.

viveka: discernment, especially between the ephemeral and eternal.

yagna: form of ritual worship in which oblations are offered into a fire according to scriptural injunctions, while sacred mantras are chanted.

yoga: 'to unite.' Union with the Supreme Being. A broad term, it also refers to the various methods of practices through which one can attain oneness with the Divine. A path that leads to Self-realization. An adept at yoga is a yogi; yogini is the female equivalent.